Christian Principles for Recovery:
For the Addicted
and those who want to help!

GOD
help me,
I can't
stop!

by

Virgil L. Stokes

Faith Christian Fellowship of Tucson
P.O. Box 89156 • Tucson, AZ 85752
E-mail: virgil@fcftucson.org • **Web Site:** www.fcftucson.org

TABLE OF CONTENTS

INTRODUCTION

I have toyed with the idea of writing this book for several years. I have even made an occasional beginning. Each beginning was quickly aborted as I recognized the time and effort required and realized my own inadequacy to do the job. It was easier to wait for someone more competent, more eloquent, or more famous to answer the call of God for this cause. In 1996 I finally gave up and started the process.

From the beginning of our ministry, my wife and I have been particularly sensitive to issues surrounding the treatment of addictions. The availability and delivery of such services at the level of the local church has been a continuing cause of concern. We have always assumed that this sensitivity was simply the natural response of two recovering alcoholics who owed their lives to the treatment community and to the availability of support groups in the community.

As time progressed we began to suspect that our background had not only sensitized us, but educated and prepared us to be of particular use in this area. Our pastoral ministry has always been marked by a high percentage of alcohol and drug abuse cases. My experience as an alcoholic and drug abuser combined with my years of employment in the treatment field gave me a foundation on which to build this ministry. We have experienced much joy in seeing amazing recoveries and felt much pain in watching good people flounder and fall.

I am especially interested in 3 groups: the minister, the alcoholic/addict, and the family.

Over our years of association with so-called "faith" ministries, we have gathered a good deal of anecdotal evidence of the need for this book. Many pastors have expressed both ignorance and interest in the subject as the Lord has given it to me. We have seen this material bring help and blessing to many addicts and their families. We have also seen ignorance of these principles bring unnecessary pain, confusion, and destruction.

There are any number of fine Christian products on the market dealing with this subject. I have used and recommended many of them. Some lean to the psychological side of the problem. Some address the issues from various theological perspectives. Many can be of value in helping those who are bound. You will find a recommended book list in the Appendix.

My aim in writing this book is to provide a straightforward assault on the pain caused by alcoholism and drug addiction as it affects the Christian, especially in the "Word" movement. I am especially interested in three groups: the minister, the alcoholic/addict, and the family. The minister needs practical information about what can realistically be done to help. The alcoholic/addict needs to know his problem and its consequences. The family needs all this information and a big dose of encouragement. I pray we are successful.

WE HAVE A MAJOR PROBLEM

PROVERBS 23:29-35

Whose heart is filled with anguish and sorrow? Who is always fighting and quarrelling? Who is the man with bloodshot eyes and many wounds? It is the one who spends long hours in the taverns, trying out new mixtures. Don't let the sparkle and the smooth taste of strong wine deceive you. For in the end it bites like a poisonous serpent; it stings like an adder. You will see hallucinations and have delirium tremens, and you will say foolish, silly things that would embarrass you no end when sober. You will stagger like a sailor tossed at sea, clinging to a swaying mast. And afterwards you will say, "I didn't even know it when they beat me up...Let's go and have another drink!

(The Living Bible)

Solomon's description of the drunk is almost humorous. In fact, many of us grew up with the notion that drunks were funny. The inebriate, and in later years the pot-head, have provided us with many a good laugh. Unfortunately, the truth of the story is considerably less amusing than the man with the lampshade on his head dancing on the piano.

Having lived through the horror of alcoholism and drug addiction, I can testify that it is not funny. I grew up around drinkers. My grandmother ran a little tavern in southern Oklahoma. I loved it there. The cowboys were nice to me, and they looked to be having a great time drinking Lone Star and Coors while they shot pool and romanced the waitress. I wanted to grow up to be just like them. At least I got the drinking part right.

I was surrounded by filth and genuine winos. How could this happen to a nice boy from the suburbs like me????

I took every opportunity to drink during my adolescent years. My parents were not drinkers, so this required a certain amount of deceit. Deceit is not a problem for an alcoholic. By the time I reached college I was committed to daily drinking. This commitment was side-tracked by an introduction to marijuana, then to other drugs. Memories of my college career are shrouded in a drug and alcohol induced fog. Somewhere in the haze, I married and divorced, graduated college, and went to work as a Registered Nurse.

My drinking and my career were in constant tension. Both were vying for my attention. It was a good fight, but after a few years, the alcohol won. I wound up in a hospital for the third time in March of 1979. This time I was really sick. I was on the verge of delirium tremens. My liver was swollen, my blood pressure explosive, and my job hanging by a thread. I was a mess. Unfortunately, my health insurance wouldn't keep me in the hospital so I was bumped to a public treatment facility in the inner city. What a shock! I was surrounded by filth and genuine winos. How could this happen to a nice boy from the suburbs?

> *My experience convinced me that psychology knows little about addiction. My church involvement gave evidence that most Christians didn't know much, either.*

By the grace of God and the help of some really wonderful people, this began my re-entry into the world of the living. My employer had mercy on me and let me return to work. I began to attend Alcoholics Anonymous meetings where I met the people who eventually introduced me to the Lord Jesus Christ. My job placed me in a position to learn a great deal about addiction. I became the Supervisor Nurse on the Drug Dependency Treatment Unit at the Veteran's Administration Hospital in Oklahoma City. My experience there convinced me that psychology knows little about addiction. My church involvement gave evidence that most Christians didn't know much, either. Unfortunately, most of my A.A. friends didn't know the Lord and were decidedly hostile to my Christian beliefs. It was all a bit distressing.

As I continued trying to help folks with alcohol and drug addictions, I became increasingly convinced that addiction is the key strategy being used by Satan to destroy our nation. When I read the headlines I see a list of woes which are attributable to addiction. Sky-rocketing health care costs, crime in the streets, and the breakdown of the family are all a by-product of addiction. Deal with the addiction problem and the others are reduced to manageable size.

In May of 1997, *Time* magazine examined the issue of addiction and its causes. J. Madeleine Nash wrote,

> *"What is not controversial is that the social cost of drug abuse, whatever its cause, is enormous. Cigarettes contribute to the death toll from cancer and heart disease. Alcohol is the leading cause of domestic violence and highway deaths. The needles used to inject heroin and cocaine are spreading aids. Directly or indirectly, addiction to drugs, cigarettes and alcohol is thought to account for a third of all hospital admissions, a quarter of all deaths and a majority of serious crimes. In the U.S. alone the combined medical and social costs of drug abuse are believed to exceed $240 billion."*

In my humble opinion this cost figure is very conservative. Health care costs alone are staggering. Former Secretary of Health, Education, and Welfare Joseph A. Califano, Jr. estimates that in 1993, the cost to society of alcohol, tobacco, and other drugs was nearly $400 billion, about $1,608 for every man, woman and child in the nation.[1]

The so-called "epidemic" of violent crime is almost entirely the offspring of chemical abuse. The vast majority of crime is committed by persons who are either intoxicated or trying to obtain money for drugs. Another large segment of the crime report is a result of drug-trafficking activities or disputes. Alcohol is a key factor in up to 68 percent of manslaughters, 62 percent of assaults, 54 percent of murders/attempted murders, 48 percent of robberies, and 44 percent of burglaries.[2] Over 60 percent of men and 50 percent of women arrested for property crimes (burglary, larceny, robbery)

> *...violent crime is almost entirely the offspring of chemical abuse.*

1   Center on Addiction and Substance Abuse, Columbia University, *The Cost of Substance Abuse to America's Health Care System, Report 1: Medicaid Hospital Costs, 1993.*

2   U.S. Department of Health and Human Services, National Institute on Alcohol Abuse and Alcoholism, Alcohol and Health: *Sixth Special Report to Congress on Alcohol and Health from the Secretary of Health and Human Services, 1987.*

in 1990, who were voluntarily tested, tested positive for illicit drug use.[1]

The cost of drugs and alcohol in the workplace is impossible to compute. Most employees are not going to tell us how much they pilfer, how often they slack off due to intoxication, and how poorly they perform when hung over. We can only guess. We know that about 70 percent of all drug users are currently employed. (Did one of them put the brakes in your car?) Up to 40 percent of industrial fatalities can be linked to alcohol consumption and alcoholism. Alcohol and drug users take three times as many sick days and are five times more likely to file worker's compensation claims than other workers.[2] Is America too stoned to compete in the world market? How much of the price of your new suit goes to pay for the derelictions of an addict?

In the face of the three-headed societal crisis of crime, health care, and fiscal collapse it seems that ignoring one common denominator in all three is inexcusable. Alcohol and drugs are at the root of crime. Eliminate addiction and street crime becomes rare again. If smoking (nicotine addiction) is included in this heading, addiction becomes far and away the leading cause of health-related expense. Business suffers and families are wrecked placing kids and moms on the public dole. Neighborhoods become war zones. It is all a result of addiction.

The barrage of statistics is endless. There are basically two possible responses. The most obvious is to bemoan the state of our society and look to government for answers it doesn't have. The other is to shout "Hallelujah!" Isn't it grand that the Lord has placed us here at a time when sin so greatly abounds? We have untold opportunity.

We are surrounded by a society flooded with alcohol and drug addicts. The jails are overflowing. The treatment centers are full. Money is tight and answers are few. Praise God, we have something to offer. Desperate people are ready to hear someone with a message of substance. Most of the treatment facilities and support groups dealing with

> *Addictions are responsible for a staggering proportion of health problems.*

1   U.S.Department of Justice, Bureau of Justice Statistics, *Drugs, Crime and the Justice System: A National Report,* Washington DC, 1992.

2   All statistics from National Clearinghouse for Alcohol and Drug Information, Alcohol, Tobacco, and Other Drugs in the Workplace. Spring, 1995. NCADI Inventory Number ML006.

addictions today are telling their clients they must establish some kind of spiritual life. They are ripe for a church which will tune in to their hearts and provide them with real answers to their spiritual questions. There is a ready-made harvest at our doorstep.

One of the first experiences we had in ministry was with a young lady in a church we pastored. She had a long history of drug addiction and alcohol usage. She had been to treatment programs and Christian counseling. Her story horrified us, but we found that hers was not an unusual case.

Her drug addiction brought her to a Charismatic church in search of answers. She gave her heart to the Lord and was wonderfully saved and filled. In the afterglow of conversion she set about to learn the Word. She discovered that she was a new creature in Christ. Armed with this information, she went to the home of

> *The question is not, "Are they here?"*
>
> *The question is, "Will you help them?"*

a leader in the church for dinner. There she was offered wine with the meal. The reasoning went something like this: "You were an addict. Now you're a new creature. You are free. Old things have passed away. Don't be bound by religion, enjoy some wine."

We were privy to the years of agony that ensued as addiction was rekindled, hope shattered, and victory lost. We met a bitter, broken woman who required years of support to get back in any condition to carry on with life. This was just the first in a line of people whose real addictions clashed with the fairy-tale theology of the churches in which they found themselves. Whether you know it or not, they and their families are in your church, some passing through, some sitting in agonized silence. The question is not, "Are they here?" The question is, "Will you help them?"

Our observation has been that most Christians, especially pastors, genuinely want to help people. Likewise, most people who come to church to get help are really looking for an answer. When our doorsteps are crowded with addicted people and their loved ones, we need all the information on the subject we can get. It is a crime to ignore the issue.

Although there are many Christian books dealing with the subject, few deal comprehensively from the perspective of the "Word" movement. We are privileged to be among those who believe that we are, in fact, new creatures in Christ. We believe:

...that the stripes of Jesus have healed us.
...that the devil must flee when we resist him.
...that drunkenness is a sin.
...that sin is to be repented of.
...that the Baptism with the Holy Ghost gives us
power to be a witness.

In addition to our theological beliefs, we have learned a few very helpful things about alcohol, drugs, and people. When interpreted in the light of the scripture, these concepts may be helpful to those who still struggle with addiction and those who strive to help them.

The first six chapters of this book dealing with the nature of the problem are for everyone. They contain general information on alcohol and addiction which will be useful to all. A chapter concerning the effects of alcoholism and addiction on family members is included. Chapters 7-12 deal with the response of the church, attempting to address the concerns of the local church, especially the clergy. It includes information on secular support groups and treatment methods, as well as suggestions for the church seeking to take an aggressive helping position toward the alcoholic/addict and his family. For those who want a practical, step-by-step guide to recovery there is an accompanying workbook entitled *"Seven Principles of Recovery: A Workbook"*. It describes practical principles for achieving wholeness. These principles will be helpful to anyone battling a life-controlling habit, such as smoking or over-eating. It is written in a workbook format and can be used by counselors and group leaders as well as their clients.

I will use the term alcoholic/addict to refer to all those who cannot, as an act of their will, cease from the ingestion of any drug. Alcohol is included as a drug. Addiction to it operates under all the same principles as addiction to any other drug. Recovery is the same for any addiction. The dynamics change slightly because of legal and social issues, but physically, spiritually, and emotionally the game is the same. Please read with an open mind and heart. I believe you will be helped.

WHAT IS ALCOHOL?

When I started this chapter, I almost called it "Identifying the Problem." Then I realized that alcohol is not the problem. Alcohol is just a thing. It has no will of its own. It bears no malice and without human cooperation is absolutely harmless. It is, on the other hand, a substance so revered that we have stores dedicated to its sale, businesses organized entirely around its consumption, and lavish advertising devoted to propagating its gospel. It is a poison so devastating that we have a unit of government assigned to its control, hospitals dedicated to recovery from its effects, and university departments resolved to study its properties.

The kind of alcohol we drink is Ethyl Alcohol, hereafter abbreviated as EtOH. It is a simple product of fermentation. By itself, it is a clear but pungent liquid. It is very flammable and an excellent solvent. When prepared for human ingestion, it is almost always resident in some other liquid which makes it palatable. Henceforth, the term "alcoholic beverage" will refer to any liquid ingested by humans which contains EtOH. This takes in the gamut from beer to wine to liquors. It will also include most cough syrups and other liquid medications, some of which are 16 percent alcohol. You really ought to read those labels before you put that stuff in your mouth.

EtOH has been a subject of discussion and a thorn in the side of man ever since Noah discovered fermentation in **GENESIS 9**. You will note that Noah immediately got drunk, got stupid, and got in trouble. This does not diagnose Noah as an alcoholic, but it does give us a glimpse of why God is so negative about drunkenness.

> *Alcohol*
> *is NOT the problem.*
>
> *It is just a thing.*

By observing the effects of alcohol any person with reasonable sense can conclude that it is a mood-altering drug. It is the most abused drug in the United States. Illicit drugs trail far behind. Whether this is due to social acceptability, legality, availability or some particular nuance of the intoxication provided, I have no idea. The important thing to remember is we are dealing with a drug of the sedative-hypnotic classification. It is a cousin to the ether used as anesthesia. It is characterized as a depressant, psychoactive, irritant which is toxic and addictive. None of these are positive attributes.

Your body is equipped to process alcohol in a very precise way. It is absorbed primarily in the small intestine. It travels in the blood to the liver where the process of detoxification begins. The alcohol molecule is changed into acetaldehyde then to acetic acid, and finally to water and oxygen to be excreted. This process takes place at the rate of about 3/4 ounce per hour, depending on size, age, and liver function. While it waits to be detoxified by the liver, the alcohol travels in the bloodstream to all parts of the body. The blood carries it to the brain where it produces most of the effects we associate with intoxication.

Alcohol

...slows reflexes,

...is an irritant which causes damage to tissue,

...acts as a desiccant: it dries things out,

...is a direct cellular poison.

Over time it causes severe damage to every body system.

The liquid in which the alcohol is hidden has no appreciable effect on the level of intoxication. The only question is how much time do you want to spend going to the restroom. A twelve ounce beer, a five ounce glass of wine, a mixed drink, or a shot glass all have about the same amount of EtOH. Each contains from 1 to 1.5 ounces. Notice that these figures exceed what the liver can handle on an hourly basis. Drink slow!

Most of the symptoms of intoxication are a result of the central nervous system effects of alcohol. EtOH in the blood crosses the blood-brain barrier and depresses your ability to think and respond from the rational mind. This means it blurs judgment and perception, accounting for the mood alteration. The normal inhibitions and anxieties that characterize rational thought and response are deadened allowing your base impulses greater freedom. Unfortunately these base impulses are drug-affected.

Alcohol also slows reflexes. This means you can't drive, walk, work, or play as well as you could sober. Unfortunately, the mood altering effects may cause you to believe that you are performing up to par. This combination can be deadly.

As with any central nervous system depressant, overdose can be a problem. As the dosage increases, the levels of consciousness affected increase as well. The effects to the cerebrum may produce giddiness. Impaired spinal reflexes cause unsteadiness, but further usage begins to affect vital sites in the brain. Just like a good sleeping pill, higher dosages proceed to unconsciousness, coma, respiratory arrest, and death. Fortunately, we usually drink alcohol at a sufficiently modest pace that we get high, get drunk, get sleepy, and get to bed before we ingest enough to kill us.

In the Fall of every year we are treated to the story of at least one poor college freshman who is "hazed" to death. In order to prove his manhood or his dedication to good old Ima Puka Psi, after an evening of drinking beer, he turns up a pint of 80 proof Old Cheapo (approximately 40 percent EtOH). His already distressed liver flies into high gear but can only manage to operate at the 1 ounce per hour rate for which it was designed. The rest of the poison goes straight to his brain where it rapidly brings him to his knees. His buddies, assuming he is simply passed out, put him in the back seat where he dies of an overdose of ethyl alcohol.

Aside from the immediate effects of intoxication and overdose, alcohol has properties which make it a long-term health problem. It is an irritant which causes damage to tissue through contact. If you have ever poured it on an open wound you know this. It kills bacteria and human cells as well. That's why it burns on the way down. It does terrible damage to your esophagus and stomach as it goes. It acts as a desiccant: it dries things out. That's why you get so thirsty when you drink. A liquid which makes you thirsty!

Beyond its simple irritant and desiccant effects, alcohol is a direct cellular poison. Over time it causes severe damage to every body system. The gastrointestinal tract becomes ulcerated. The liver loses cells and forms scar tissue until it literally becomes hard. This is cirrhosis of the liver. Brain and nerve cells are destroyed until thought is clouded, reflexes shot, and bodily functions are out of control. Alcohol is not a kind killer.

Probably most interesting to our purpose here is the fact that EtOH is addictive. Regular use will lend itself to psychological and physical dependence.

Alcohol is addictive

Psychological dependence means we get in the habit of using it for the purpose of relieving emotional discomfort or performing some other desirable function. When we try to quit we experience anxiety, depression, and irritability. We miss our friend. We are psychologically dependent when we feel we need alcohol in order to perform some function in our life.

Continued regular use will result in a positive cellular craving for the drug. This means there has been an actual chemical change in the cells of our body which now requires EtOH to function normally. Removal of the drug brings physical withdrawal symptoms. These may range from what drunks call "the inner shakes" to full-scale delirium tremens. Tremulousness, nausea, agitation, and sleeplessness are early symptoms. Continued use may result in muscle spasms, convulsions, hallucinations, and even death.

While it would be fun to spend some time talking about the evils of alcohol in general, I'm going to pass that opportunity for now and focus on those who are in the dependent category. These are the people to whom we refer when we use the term "alcoholic." Let's identify our problem person.

WHAT IS ALCOHOLISM?

The time has come to make a request for tolerance. The following discussion will at times be offensive to some readers. I beseech you to read it all before you get mad and quit. Particularly offended will be the religiously indoctrinated who see alcoholics as weak-willed and purposefully sinful. Please! I am as committed to conviction, repentance, and restoration as the next person. Trust me.

Before we define the word "alcoholism," let's do a quick test. Words have meaning. Unfortunately, they don't always mean the same thing to everybody. Our perception of a term is colored by our experience, education, and training. When I hear the word "dog" I see in my mind a little brown and white mutt. He was my dog when I was a kid. You probably picture some other dog. The term has very positive connotations to me. He was my buddy and playmate for years. To you, the term might conjure memories of pain, fear, filth or any number of other unpleasant associations.

The same is true of the word "alcoholic." Many folks think of a particular person of their acquaintance. If that person is one with unpleasant associations, then the term may evoke violent response. Many people picture scruffy, stinky winos and recoil with contempt. When I hear the term I see a room full of working people, all drinking coffee and laughing as they prepare for a meeting of Alcoholics Anonymous. The word has different meanings to different people. The same is true of the term "addict." It means many things to many people. What is the picture in your mind when you hear these words? It would be helpful if you would lay aside your preconceptions and allow us to standardize our terms.

> *What is the picture in your mind when you hear the term "addict"?*

We will use the term "alcoholism" to refer to dependency on the drug alcohol. Included in the definition will be all the physical, psychological, social, mental, and emotional ramifications of that dependency. This dependency may be psychological or physical or both. The characteristics common to dependency on alcohol define a syndrome. A syndrome is any set of characteristics regarded as identifying a certain type or condition. Alcoholism has a set of common characteristics which make up the "syndrome" of alcoholism. We need to learn a few things about these characteristics.

The American Medical Association began referring to alcoholism as a disease in the 1950's. This designation makes most evangelical Christians very nervous, and not without good reason. It seems to absolve the individual from responsibility for his actions and turn him into a poor victim of fate. Please don't let the term bother you. Think of addiction as a syndrome. It is simply a recognizable cluster of symptoms, or characteristics, with a predictable outcome which serve to identify a particular condition. It gives us a way to identify the people we are referring to when we say "alcoholic" or "addict." We will deal with the sin issue shortly.

One of the earliest attempts to identify alcoholism as a disease came in the 1930's. A New York physician named Silkworth became involved in the treatment of a number of seemingly hopeless cases. His observations of these hapless fellows prompted him to describe the syndrome as "an allergy of the body combined with an obsession of the mind". He recognized a phenomenon that would take decades to explain: The alcoholic has a craving for alcohol which is triggered by the ingestion of the drug. One drink prompts a drive for the next. This craving is never experienced by the non-alcoholic drinker. This is key to an understanding of the experience of the alcoholic, or any addict, and will help to discern between the alcoholic and the heavy drinker.[1]

The ensuing years have revealed several characteristics of alcoholism which help describe the syndrome. If you suspect you may have a drinking problem you will want to read these next paragraphs very carefully. If you care about an alcoholic you simply must familiarize yourself with these facts. Alcoholism as we will address it is primary, progressive, chronic, selective, tri-partite, and treatable. I want to discuss each of these characteristics.

Alcoholism is Primary Progressive Chronic Selective Tri-partite and Treatable.

---

1   *Alcoholics Anonymous,* **Third Edition (Alcoholics Anonymous World Services, Inc, New York City, 1976). Pg. xxvi (Paraphrased by author from "The Doctor's Opinion")**

PRIMARY

In medical jargon, the term "primary" refers to a condition which takes priority in treatment. Picture a man coming to an emergency room after an automobile accident. He has a broken arm. This surely needs to be treated. Unfortunately, he has also punctured an artery and is bleeding profusely. The emergency room doctor would be a fool to set the broken arm before he stops the bleeding. The bleeding artery is a primary condition. If he doesn't treat the artery, the broken arm won't matter.

One of the first things that usually happens to an alcoholic when he comes in contact with the health care system is referral for psychiatric evaluation. We rational people see his behavior and assume he must be insane. We hear his complaints and assume he is depressed. Unfortunately, if he doesn't stop drinking we are doing cognitive therapy with a cognitively impaired person. We are trying to reason with an unreasonable man. It is entirely possible, even likely, that his mental condition and most of his physical maladies are a by-product of his drinking. We have to stop the bleeding before we can reasonably treat any other condition. In other words, don't let the drinking kill you while you try to analyze your childhood.

Let me make myself perfectly clear. No matter what you think or what the alcoholic tells you, his primary problem is alcoholism. Do not be deterred by smoke screens of emotional upset, phantom physical problems, or anything else that might postpone the necessity to do the obvious. If he needs emergency medical treatment, do it. But if he doesn't

> *No matter what you think or what the alcoholic tells you, his PRIMARY problem is alcoholism.*

stop drinking you are simply postponing the inevitable. I say this very emphatically because it is so easy to allow yourself to be fooled by these expert manipulators. He is not drunk because he is depressed. He is depressed because he keeps getting drunk. Stop the drinking for six months. You will be amazed at the number of other difficulties which disappear.

PROGRESSIVE

A progressive condition is one which, without intervention in the process, will continue to get worse until the predictable end is reached. In the

> *A progressive condition is one which will continue to get worse until the predictable end is reached.*

case of alcoholism, the outcome is death unless incarceration or incapacitation comes first. The alcoholic dies ten to twelve years younger than his peer group. For some, this wouldn't be so bad if they didn't die so ugly. An alcoholic death is generally very cruel.

The latter stages of alcoholism are marked by all manner of mental and physical breakdowns. The digestive tract is ulcerated by the continued use of the irritant. Ulcers, colitis, and chronic malnutrition are typical. Needless to say, the liver suffers. As the disease progresses the organ first swells, then shrinks and hardens as tissue is irrevocably destroyed. This causes many problems in other systems. The blood pressure goes up, the kidneys begin to fail, the heart begins to weaken from over work. In the esophagus, little blood vessels begin to swell and finally burst causing hemorrhage. The central nervous system begins to show signs of severe deterioration: a shuffling gait, memory lapses, mental confusion, and even dementia.

For others, the disease never progresses to these extremes. Some find their way to prison due to crimes committed in service to their disease. Some become so mentally impaired they wind up in institutions. I'll leave you to decide which is the more fortunate. Thankfully, some recognize the problem before they reach these end-stage conditions and take appropriate action. This is a disease that gives itself away by many symptoms as it works in a person.

The earliest symptoms are largely subjective and often go unnoticed. The person drinking alcoholically starts like all of us. He drinks to experience an upswing in mood, a mild euphoria. As he learns to take advantage of this benefit, he begins to experience a downswing in mood after episodes of drinking. He learns that this pain can be treated with another drink (substitute pill, or cigarette, or whatever). He has begun to drink for relief of distress. This is not good.

As time wears on, relief drinking gives way to maintenance drinking. Distress has become the usual feeling level. It is interrupted by drinking which no longer serves to bring the addict up to mild euphoria or intoxication. He is now drinking only to feel normal. This individual is in serious trouble, yet may remain undetected by others for years. The progression continues until drinking no longer brings him to normal. He drinks in an obsessive but futile attempt to be free from pain. His relief comes only when unconscious. Oblivion is the best he can do. Now he is obvious to all who know him.

Along with the progression from normal to relief to maintenance to obsession to oblivion, there occur many other side effects. For the purposes of identification, let me put together a list of symptoms in some semblance of order of severity. This is not a formula for a downward slide, one symptom following diagnostically after the previous. It is never that orderly. But each one is a signpost marking a path which is unmistakable and proceeds inevitably to the same end:

> • *An increase in tolerance: it takes more chemical to get high.*

> • *Blackouts begin: periods of time are lost while drinking, though the individual remains awake. This is a chemically induced amnesia. It may be moments, then minutes, then whole evenings, etc.*

> • *Guilt about drinking: this begins the necessity to sneak drinks, lie about intake, and make up reasons (excuses) to drink.*

> • *Personal attempts at control: playing little mind games to try to cut down. Only drink beer. Never drink on Tuesday. No one else may ever know this is going on.*

> • *Attempts at geographical change: may try moving, changing jobs, changing bars, changing wives. Nothing works.*

> • *Promises and resolutions followed by repeated failures.*

> • *Deterioration of social context: avoiding family and friends, finding companions who drink in the same way. Planning all activities around the availability of the intoxicant. Anyone who makes consistent choices concerning important activities based on this issue is in serious danger.*

The disease continues in the body even during periods of abstinence.

As the syndrome winds to its end and the intake becomes excessive, all these things multiply. We see chronic addiction.

> • *Tremors, sometimes accompanied with morning drinking or tranquilizer use.*

- *Vague, indefinable fears. Sleep impairment. Night terrors and sweats.*

- *A loss of outside interests. Business and job suffer badly.*

- *Deterioration of the moral standard accompanied by constant remorse and depression. The addict does things he would never do when not driven by his addiction. He may steal at the job, fail to provide for his family, or demonstrate violent behavior totally inconsistent with his pre-morbid character.*

- *A decrease in tolerance: unconsciousness or blackout now comes after only one or two drinks.*

- *Unreasonable resentment and hostility. Mental deterior-ation. Memory impairment and paranoia. Logic is difficult. Paranoia is not uncommon.*

- *Dietary neglect.*

- *Physical breakdown.*

A person who is having difficulties in life associated with drinking but does not stop or alter his drinking behavior is likely to have a problem. Remember, once the person has begun the trip down the road to destruction there is no turning back. The disease continues in the body even during periods of abstinence. To return to drinking is to return to addiction is to progress to destruction.

CHRONIC

Addictions are not only progressive, they are also chronic. This may seem a fine line of differentiation, but it is important to single out and identify this characteristic. While "progressive" means that the condition always gets worse, "chronic" implies that it never goes away. The chronicity of alcoholism has given rise to the old Alcoholics Anonymous saying that this disease is very patient. It's always there waiting for you if you fall off the wagon.

Because of this aspect of the syndrome, it is impossible for the alcoholic person to ever successfully drink in moderation. The tables of A.A. meetings around the world are peopled with individuals who have tried every conceivable method to learn to control their drug. The stories are endless. My wife's father was an alcoholic who remained sober in Alcoholics Anonymous for over 15 years. When he began to drink again he immediately sank to levels below his previous bottom. This time he lost his family, and within three years he lost his life.

This is a controversial concept. There are many in the treatment professions who would have us believe that an addict can learn to control his intake. It is simply a matter of behavioral modification. Joining these people in their theory are any number of addicts who sincerely want to believe this fiction. Certainly there are those who manage to drink with a degree of moderation after showing signs of alcoholism at earlier periods. I think there are two reasons for this.

One group of people who find it possible to moderate their intake are those who were never genuinely addicted in the first place. These individuals are what we would classify as heavy drinkers. They may have been bad actors, but they have not become addicted to alcohol. This means that when the drug is introduced into their body they do not experience craving. In their younger days they simply enjoyed the experience of intoxication and all the hoopla that accompanied it. When the repercussions of that behavior became too great, they managed to control their intake.

The other group of individuals who seem to fit the "learned-control" model are those who are very good at their alcoholism. They have managed to fool themselves and/or their therapists, and are giving the impression of a normal life.

> *This disease is very patient. "Chronic" implies it never goes away.*

This is one of the primary modes of existence for every alcoholic. To think they could fool a researcher, especially a researcher with an agenda, is certainly not far-fetched. The real diagnostic question is not "Are they drinking less then a prescribed amount per week?" but "Are they thinking about drinking an inordinate amount of the day?" It is not so much the intake of the drug, but the amount of mental, spiritual, and emotional energy expended in control that diagnoses an addict when not involved in a binge. A normal person does not have to try to stay sober.

The two-edged sword of alcoholism is a mental obsession coupled with a physical craving. An alcoholic, even when not drinking, devotes a high percentage of his thought life to alcohol. He watches the clock to see when he can expect a drink. He plans his lunch, his recreation, and his bedtime to fit his addictive schedule. He is fascinated with the chemical and its effects. After the initial phase of detoxification, most of treatment is dedicated to battling this obsession of the mind. Real sobriety leads us to a place in our thought life which is alcohol free. My mind is so changed that today I am not an alcoholic trying to stay sober or control my intake. I am a human who does not choose to drink.

Physical craving is the aspect of addiction which never changes. No matter how long an alcoholic stays dry, when the drug enters the system the addict begins to experience a drive to ingest more. I have found this very difficult to explain to those who have never experienced it. It is often accompanied by increased anxiety, tachycardia (rapid pulse), diaphoresis (sweating), and obsessive thinking. No matter how long an addict has been drug free, the ingestion of intoxicants will trigger craving. This phenomenon can also be triggered at times by visual, auditory, or olfactory stimuli. This tells us that there is a degree of conditioning involved, but there is definitely a physical response in the addict.

One morning several years ago my wife was so kind as to prepare a breakfast drink for me. It was one of those liquid breakfast kind of things. I sloshed it down as I prepared to go to the church. I was an Assistant Pastor. An ordained minister. I had been sober for several years and rarely even thought about drinking. It was no longer part of my life.

As I showered, a remarkable thing happened. My neck veins distended. My heart rate increased and my pulse throbbed audibly in my head. I was short of breath and sweaty. I felt shaky. My belly was hosting a butterfly convention. When I got out of the shower I called to my wife, "If I didn't know better, I'd say I was craving a drink!" As we prayed and pondered what was happening, Judy thought to check the ingredients in the breakfast drink. She found that I had ingested a small amount of alcohol in the form of banana extract. Minuscule but deadly. I thank God I was built up in the Lord.

This is a reaction that a "normal" person never has. It has nothing to do with willpower or character or any of the things we normally associate with drunks and their derelictions. It has to do with a physical response to the ingestion of a chemical. Had I not been built up in the Word of God and knowledgeable about the nature of alcoholism, I would have been a prime candidate for a relapse. Instead, I spoke to the symptoms in the Name of Jesus and my body returned to normal.

About two years later, addiction showed its staying power again. I was washing dishes when I glanced at the television in the living room. On screen was a very graphic scene of a junkie injecting himself with heroin. When I saw the image of his blood backing up into the syringe, registering that he was in the vein, I immediately began to salivate heavily and tasted the distinct bitterness of quinine. This sensation, familiar to all heroin users, was one I had not experienced since my last heroin injection many years before. The addictive memory of my mind and body has not gone away.

From a biblical standpoint this makes abundant good sense. Jesus outlined the principle in **MATTHEW 12:43-45**.

> *"When a defiling evil spirit is expelled from someone, it*
> *drifts along through the desert looking for an oasis, some*
> *unsuspecting soul it can bedevil. When it doesn't find*
> *anyone, it says, 'I'll go back to my old haunt.' On return it*
> *finds the person spotlessly clean, but vacant. It then runs*
> *out and rounds up seven other spirits more evil than itself*
> *and they all move in, whooping it up. That person ends up*
> *far worse off than if he'd never gotten cleaned up in the first*
> *place. "That's what this generation is like: You may think*
> *you have cleaned out the junk from your lives and gotten*
> *ready for God, but you weren't hospitable to my kingdom*
> *message, and now all the devils are moving back in."*

(Message Bible)

He notes that when an evil spirit goes out of a man, it always returns to see if there is anybody home. If the spirit determines that the outside of the man has been cleaned up, but that the inside is still empty, he then moves back in with seven of his demonic buddies. We have a guarantee from Jesus that if we drink again we will get worse. We can also see the necessity of putting something on the inside, not just cleaning up the outside.

Because of the chronic nature of addiction, I purposely avoid ingesting food or drink which is alcohol based. This includes mouthwash and medications of all kinds. It also means we don't cook with alcohol. There is no reason to intentionally place ourselves in harm's way. Any mood-altering chemical can be dangerous for the addict. The drunk should avoid tranquilizers and the addict must avoid alcohol. Cross-addiction is very common. In the case of prescription drugs, especially pain killers of a narcotic type, great care must be exercised. In case of surgery or injury, it is wise to enlist a fellow Christian, preferably an addict in recovery, who can monitor the use of drugs to help us stay on the prescribed regimen. When the addiction tastes the drug, it often prompts us to lie to ourselves and rationalize compulsive use as being therapeutic.

SELECTIVE

Alcoholism selects its victims. We don't know exactly how, but we know it does. Equal drinking does not mean equal problems. Some will drink heavily at certain periods of life then stop or moderate as the demands of time and circumstance change. Others who match them drink for drink will progress down the slide to total immersion in alcoholism. Addiction to other drugs seems to follow the same pattern.

During my college days I ran with a group of hard drinkers and druggers. Sure there were danger signs in my drinking, such as a reputation for a large capacity for alcohol, but by and large my whole crew drank hard. As college days passed and careers began, most of those other fellows put the bottle down and took up the trappings of responsible lives. A few of us, however, continued to drink and take drugs while trying to carry on in the world of work and family. We failed.

Why some become alcoholic and others do not is open to debate. We know there is a genetic factor. Some are simply more susceptible to alcohol addiction than others. There are undoubtedly social and cultural factors as well. Remember, if there is alcoholism in your family you are more likely to be alcoholic if you decide to drink. Note that last phrase, "...IF you decide to drink." *__If you don't drink you won't be an alcoholic.__* I believe it is important to arm kids with these facts. Sometimes good information will help them make good decisions when all our sermons fail.

Equal drinking does not mean equal problems

Another aspect of the selectiveness of addiction is that there is no amount of drinking or frequency of usage which defines who becomes addicted. Many subjective reports indicate there are those who were hooked from their earliest experiences. Others drink moderately for years then succumb to alcoholism after retirement. The cruel truth is you never know until it is too late. You can never know if or when it will take control, but once it does you can never turn back. The only completely safe choice is abstinence.

TRI-PARTITE

As Christians we know man is a three-part being. We are spirit, created in the image of God who is spirit. We abide in a physical body created by God out of the dust of the ground. Animating our existence is a mental/emotional realm

> *Addiction attacks a person on 3 levels: Spirit, Soul, and Body*

which we call the soul. Addiction is a condition which attacks a person on all three levels. This concept is crucial to effective recovery.

Everybody recognizes the physical aspects of alcoholism. As we have previously described, alcohol, and all addictive drugs, have ongoing destructive effects on the human body. In addition, addiction is itself a physical phenomenon. It is the result of changes in the chemistry of the body.

While there is some argument as to the exact nature of the problem, nearly all will grant that the addict has mental and emotional difficulties. Speaking from a Christian perspective, we can clearly identify several. First note that the soul of man is comprised of his thoughts, his feelings, and his will. All three are grievously affected by alcoholism.

God has given man a wonderful set of mental tools which psychology has dubbed "defense mechanisms." When functioning normally, these marvelous mental safety valves allow us to endure great distress with rosy dispositions, attack insurmountable odds with enthusiasm, and respond instinctively to protect ourselves and our loved ones from harm. The addict, however, has taken these tools and twisted their use to protect his addiction. He attacks his friends, and behaves with cowardice while his family is destroyed before his eyes, yet he is unable to see his part in the process.

One mark of an addict is his obsession with his drug. His thoughts are preoccupied with it most of his waking hours. He plans his life around his relationship with it. Vacation plans, job prospects, and recreational events are screened according to their effect on his drug use. Thought must be given to maintaining the supply. Store hours, holiday intrusions, and transportation problems all must be taken into account. All sources of possible supply must be mentally indexed and classified according to quality and reliability. It really is a full-time occupation, or should I say pre-occupation.

A favorite weapon of the addict is rationalization. This is the mental process of taking an excuse and turning it into a reason. The addict is able to convince himself, and often everybody else, that his behavior is easily explainable. It couldn't have been drinking that caused him to forget to pick up his daughter after school. It was actually the stress of his job. A lesser man would probably fold under the pressure, he rationalizes. Instead, he just has a little drink to let off steam. The excuses and alibis of any addict could fill volumes. The weather, the Cowboys, the President, and life in general give open permission to imbibe and be absolved from consequences. The dangerous thing is, he actually believes it. That's why he can be so convincing when he lies to others.

Projection is probably the best offensive weapon in the arsenal. This means that I feel or think something which I don't find acceptable. Rather than recognize my attitude, I ascribe it to you. It's so much easier to hate you than it is to hate myself. I lost my job. You are irresponsible. I punched the boss. You are an angry person. Projection is first cousin to displacement, which means getting mad at the Boss, but punching you. These two run together in a partnership whose primary objective is to make everyone else feel crazy while I feel sane. If you are feeling guilty for someone else's behavior, you have been duped. Check it out!

> **DENIAL**
> **is the ability**
> **to look truth squarely**
> **in the eye**
> **and call it a lie.**

Denial is the granddaddy of all defense mechanisms for the alcoholic. It is the one that marks him. It is the one that kills him. It is the ability to look truth squarely in the eye and call it a lie. This is a normal stage in any terminal disease. Everyone goes through it. The bad news comes and we don't want to believe it. It's too awful. The alcoholic sees the results of his condition, examines all the facts, listens to all the testimony, and in the face of overwhelming evidence to the contrary, pronounces himself "OK." The depth of his ability to ignore the obvious is beyond the scope of normal people to understand. They are baffled by the addict's behavior.

Breaking down denial is a primary focus of hospital treatment for addiction. If nothing else is accomplished in a thirty-day treatment program, we have been successful if the addict begins to take responsibility for his problem. This is why the folks get so excited when someone says for the first time, "I'm an alcoholic." It means there is hope. The only way to start on the right road is to admit you're on the wrong one.

It is important to note that when denial is truly broken, some sort of emotional response is to be expected. Reality is that a death sentence has been pronounced which can only be avoided by a radical change in lifestyle. A smiling nod of the head is not normal. This type of mild reaction probably means he is trying to be polite until you shut up and he can drink again. The alcoholic has an internal "Yes, but..." tape catalog which plays constantly to counter every rational argument. It is this ability to deny the obvious that spawned A.A.'s traditional meeting greeting, "Hi, I'm Wino and I'm an alcoholic." The mental postscript being, "And I don't ever want to forget it."

Beyond the bizarre thinking that attends the disease, the soul is also affected in the emotional area. Fear and resentment mark the emotional lives of every addict. Both of these boogie men have their roots in the spiritual condition. One who is spiritually fit finds himself obeying the command of love delivered to the church by the Lord Jesus. This certainly precludes harboring bitterness and allows the wonder of **1 JOHN 4:18** to become real in the believer's life.

> *There is no room in love for fear. Well-formed love banishes fear. Since fear is crippling, a fearful life – fear of death, fear of judgment – is one not yet fully formed in love.*

> (Message Bible)

In spite of their spiritual root, fear and resentment are experienced as emotions, and we will talk about them as such.

Resentment is one of the alcoholic's real talents. We can carry a grudge over the smallest slight for years. We can take the insignificant and unintended, roll it around in our minds, wrap it in rationalization, and present it to the world as malice well-deserved. Grudges, gripes and vengeance occupy a good part of the drunk's emotional life. I remember distinctly sitting in a drug-induced stupor and proclaiming with the pseudo-intellectual's disdain for difference, "The only real emotions are hatred and fear." In actuality, they were the only ones I was capable of feeling at the time.

Fear, of course, is something an addict should be feeling. He is facing insanity, incarceration, or death. He has usually committed any number of crimes which may catch up to him at any moment. Unfortunately, he is rarely afraid of the right things. As the disease progresses, he simply feels a general distrust of life. Fear may gnaw at his belly night and day, but he would be hard-pressed to tell you what he is afraid of. His pride would probably insist he not talk about it at all.

When I was just a few weeks sober I spoke to my sponsor about the fear I felt day and night. It attacked me in the night and swept over me in waves during the day. It was never totally out of my consciousness. At times I thought I would scream. At other times I wanted to double over from the pain in my gut. My sponsor asked what I was afraid of. I said I didn't know. He smiled knowingly and said, "Oh, good! You're afraid of IT. We're all afraid of IT. Don't worry. IT will go away." What a relief!

There is a long list of other emotional distresses which addicts may experience. Most are emotionally labile, their moods shifting abruptly and without warning. Many are depressed, experiencing long bouts with hopelessness and self-pity. Much of this emotional volatility will dissipate with sobriety as the mind and body recover from the rebound effects of intoxication. Others, especially those who began using drugs or drinking at early ages, may actually go through the emotions associated with adolescence. There will be a period of learning all the life lessons that should have been learned in a sober maturation process. This can be quite uncomfortable at times.

In addition to the thoughts and emotions, the soul of man is also affected in the area of the will. This is the realm which genuinely sanctifies man as the crown of God's creation. Man is the only creature with the power to decide his own destiny. He is not at the mercy of his impulses. He can decide, make choices about his actions. God bestowed upon man the dignity of determining his own eternity. When a human being repeatedly gives away his power to decide his actions by dulling his faculties with a drug, that holy power is lost to him. He no longer enjoys the dignity of choosing whether to drink or not.

In **JOHN 8:31-32**, Jesus uttered the famous line about the truth making us free.

> *Then Jesus turned to the Jews who had claimed to believe in Him. If you stick with this, living out what I tell you, you are My disciples for sure. Then you will experience for yourselves the truth. The truth will free you.*

(Message Bible)

These words were spoken to people who had already believed in Jesus, yet they were apparently not yet free. Notice freedom comes only after a period of continuing in the Word of Christ. When we first believe we are not aware of much truth, much less able to apply it successfully. It is only after we walk with the Lord for a while that truth begins to dawn on us and we begin to understand freedom. Freedom is simply the power to choose.

For the alcoholic, freedom begins with the power to choose not to drink. He has given this choice away. God restores it to him. This wonderful freedom usually takes time to be fully enjoyed. In the beginning the addict in recovery may only be able to choose to come to meetings where others will help him make other right choices. He may need the support of a loving peer group to assist him in continuing in the Word until the truth finally dawns on him. He may need a friend who will recognize that his failures are not the result of a lack of sincerity or a lack of willpower, but are the result of a lack of truth. Freedom takes time.

From the spiritual standpoint the alcoholic is in the same condition as anyone who lives in a manner contrary to the dictates of his conscience. He is alienated from God. From a theological perspective, the alcoholic needs the same thing any person needs: He must be born from above. Jesus said very clearly that any person who wishes to see the kingdom of God must be reborn by the divine work of the Holy Spirit (JOHN 3:3-7).

> *Jesus answered, "I am telling you the truth: no one can see the Kingdom of God without being born again." "How can a grown man be born again?" Nicodemus asked. "He certainly cannot enter his mother's womb and be born a second time!" "I am telling you the truth," replied Jesus, "that no one can enter the Kingdom of God without being born of water and the Spirit. A person is born physically of human parents, but is born spiritually of the Spirit. Do not be surprised because I tell you that you must all be born again."*

(Good News Bible)

We are universally in need of a change on the inside. It is the human condition.

Unfortunately, many a drunk has come to the altar to pray the sinner's prayer and pledge his allegiance to Christ only to find himself soon overwhelmed with living problems which drive him to relapse. The church is often wont to dismiss him as insincere in his conversion or a backslider who was simply not strong enough to resist temptation. At best he is tolerated and pitied. At worst he is vilified. He needs more than a perfunctory altar session to live a sober life.

Beyond the general need for regeneration which results from being human, the alcoholic has some specific difficulties. He has been living under the control of a drug which has allowed him to commit many acts of omission and commission which are contrary to the convictions in his heart. The alcoholic lives with a terrible load of guilt. He drinks to quiet it, rationalizes to assuage it, and rails at the persons he has harmed most. The realization that he needs to be forgiven is a crucial step in beginning his recovery.

Having recognized his wrongdoing, the alcoholic must move from self-recrimination to the reception of forgiveness. This first requires believing and receiving the grace of God to forgive. Then the process of restoring broken human relationships must be undertaken. Finally, the alcoholic must somehow come to the point of forgiving himself. Out of this three-branched root system of forgiveness and reconciliation springs the love of God, love of others, and love of self which banishes fear and resentment. This takes time and nurture in an environment which recognizes the danger and the tragedy of relapse.

The condition of alcoholism or addiction affects all three parts of a person. The effects are deep, and must be addressed in order for wholeness to result. Any system of treatment which does not address all three is doomed to failure. Simply removing the alcohol is insufficient. The treatment professions have spent decades trying to treat addicts with mental and physical cures. Nearly all now recognize the necessity to address the spiritual realm as well. It is my sincere hope that the church can be as wise in recognizing the need for physical and mental support.

TREATABLE

Alcoholism is a condition which is treatable. We know how to help the person who seeks help. There are effective programs all over the country with high rates of success. The problem is the treatment only works on those who are treated. Unlike most diseases, the alcoholic is not running to the emergency room crying, "Help!" Instead, he is busy trying to explain away the obvious symptoms of his condition. This is normal. As noted above, it is actually a part of the mental aberration caused by the disease itself.

This is truly sad and deadly. Most experts tell us that only about one in ten who are alcoholic ever seek treatment on their own. This shouldn't be too surprising. We have a disease which clouds the mind by its very nature. The denial of its own existence is one of its primary symptoms. Yet many times we look at the fellow who is suffering and shake our heads in wonder that he can't see his condition. We are asking an irrational, blinded person to make a rational, informed decision.

Treatment involves addressing all three levels of the illness. We first must confront the denial which prevents treatment. Then the physical addiction must be addressed along with the physical conditions caused by abuse. Finally, the mental, emotional, and spiritual difficulties must be corrected. Recovery from the ravages of alcoholism and addiction is a process, not a place. A process requires commitment, support, and patience.

> *IMPORTANT!*
> *Alcoholism*
> *is treatable.*

We know this condition kills. We know how to recognize it. We know how to treat it. We know that the alcoholic will probably not get better on his own. I believe it is incumbent upon those who care for him to inform themselves, then pray for wisdom and courage in finding ways to apply loving pressure to force a crisis. This is uncomfortable. Mama told us we should mind our own business. If we love someone who is out of control, it is our business. Looking the other way is tantamount to manslaughter for the sake of decorum.

Recovery from the ravages of alcoholism and addiction is a process, not a place. A process requires commitment, support and patience.

SOME THINGS ALCOHOLISM IS NOT

If you are one of those who has trouble using the word "disease" to describe alcoholism, I want to thank you for indulging me thus far. Before I enter deeper into that perilous terrain, there are a few popular misconceptions which need to be debunked. Most of our preconceptions are actually misconceptions. Many ideas are based on prejudices or faulty information imparted by parents, teachers, media, or friends. I find that these are often most easily uprooted when directly addressed.

Alcoholism is NOT the result of a faulty upbringing. The vast majority of alcoholics are middle class or above. They come from homes indistinguishable from other homes. Many were raised in church. Many are well-educated, well-mannered, and well-bred. There are certainly environmental factors involved. The family attitude toward drinking probably has a bearing. The general availability of parental oversight makes a difference, but the difference is in the timing of the first drink, not in the development of alcoholism.

This is important. It is important for the non-alcoholic to understand that alcoholics are people from every social class. There is no room for looking down on them as some sort of inferior product of evolution. For parents of alcoholics it is important to know that blame does not lie in some heinous developmental misdeed. It's not because you hugged too little, laughed too much, or dropped him on his head. These may have caused all kinds of other neuroses and personality quirks, but it did not make him an alcoholic.

Alcoholism is NOT the result of an "addictive personality." This was the fantasy of most of the treatment community when I was in college. We had piles of literature attempting to describe devious, over-dependent, obsessive people who were addicted to one drug or the other. The idea was that we could identify these folks ahead of time and try to prevent them from becoming addicted. This would be very convenient if only it were true.

What we find, however, is that addicts come from every personality type. Happy people get addicted. Sour people get addicted. Strong people, weak people, mean people, kind people. The truth is that certain characteristics routinely develop as a result of addiction. They don't cause it, it causes them. Addicts in general are dependent, resentful, deceitful, self-centered, and secretive. No matter how they start out, this is what they become.

The development of addiction progresses very much like any relationship. The addict becomes increasingly immersed in his relationship with his drug. This alters all the other relationships in his life. It is really a love story. There is a time of initiating acquaintance, finding out that this relationship is pleasurable. There is a period of mental obsession. The addict is not high all the time, but his thoughts are consumed with fantasies of being with his new lover. The affair progresses to the "going steady" stage. All activities are centered around the drug. Any person or activity that interferes with that priority must be put away. Any person who dares question the wisdom of this union is immediately vilified. There comes the time when a full commitment is made. Life is inextricably intertwined with the drug. It pervades every thought, every activity, and every attitude. Life's plans must include the partner. We are one. For better or....

Alcoholism ...is NOT the result of faulty upbringing ...is NOT the result of an "addictive personality" ...is NOT a moral problem

Unfortunately, alcohol is a lousy lover. As the marriage continues, the thrill diminishes. We go to all the old places and do all the same things, but the joy is gone. By the time we wake up to realize that our lover is trying to kill us, we have usually alienated everyone who would be likely to give us support in what will be a messy divorce. It becomes a marriage of desperation. I can't live with it, and I can't comprehend life without it.

This model of a developing, deepening relationship is helpful in understanding the attitudes of the alcoholic as well as in recognizing addictive thinking early in the process. I am no longer hurt by the defensiveness of the addict. I am not surprised when he sneaks and lies. When he forgets important appointments because his mind is awash with alcoholic dreams, fears and fantasies, I shrug. I understand when he avoids family gatherings. My antenna perks up when I hear of someone who loses a job because of his drinking, but blames his unfair employer. These are all simply symptoms of a predictable, progressive process.

Alcoholism is NOT a moral problem. It does not indicate a lack of character or willpower. It may precipitate moral problems. It may destroy character and erode willpower. But it is not a moral problem. Anyone who gets drunk is likely to do or say immoral things. This does not make them alcoholic. It makes them immoral. There are fine, decent people who become alcoholic. There are also real jerks who become alcoholic. They are both equally alcoholic, but not equally moral. In the next chapter I will deal at some length with the issue of the sinfulness of alcoholism. In the meantime, let us understand that we are not necessarily dealing with evil, immoral people. Sitting in the seat of judgment puts us in a poor position to extend a helping hand.

CHAPTER FIVE
BUT IS IT A SIN OR A DISEASE?

We might as well cut to the chase. In most treatment programs, it is commonly accepted that alcoholism, or any addiction, is a disease. In the church, especially in the Fundamentalist or Charismatic, Bible-believing variety, it is widely assumed to be a sin. Both positions have considerable merit and are understandable based on the perspective of those who hold them. Let's see if we can locate the truth of the matter.

It has been my privilege to be exposed to all sides of the argument in a most personal way. By age thirty I was a full-fledged alcoholic and drug addict in the final spiral toward destruction. I found my way to treatment and to support group meetings. In the context of those meetings I became acquainted with Christian people who led me into a new relationship with the Lord. I had the opportunity to work in the treatment field with adults and adolescents, and then sensed a call to Bible school. Since that time I have been in full-time ministry, including many years in pastoral ministry. I hope I have some perspective on the question.

> *The American Medical Association has categorized it (alcoholism) as a disease since the 1950's.*

It seems to me that most of the argument between the "disease concept" people and the "repent and be delivered" people is one of terminology and perspective. Based on much of the information we have already presented about the physical, psychological, and sociological effects of alcoholism, the American Medical Association has categorized it as a disease since the 1950's. According to the A.M.A. alcoholism is:

> *"...an illness that is characterized by significant impairment in the emotional, psychological, spiritual, physical, and social areas that is directly associated with the persistent and excessive use of alcohol. Impairment may involve psychological or social dysfunction. Alcoholism also is manifested as a type*

of drug dependence of pathological extent and pattern, which ordinarily interferes seriously with the patient's mental and physical health and his adaptation to his environment."[1]

I don't know a single alcoholic who can't say "Amen!" to that.

When we use words they have meaning to each of us individually. The trick to communication is in using words to describe concepts which have the same meaning to all involved in the discussion. The word "disease" is no different. Your idea of a disease may be different from mine, which is different from Pastor Straightarrow's at the First Church, which in turn is likely to be different from Dr. Firewater's at the Booze-No-More Treatment Center. It would probably help our debate if we all meant the same thing when we said "disease."

Webster's New World Dictionary, Second College Edition, says a disease is, **"any departure from health, or...a particular destructive process in an organ or organism, with a specific cause and characteristic symptoms."**[2]

From the point of view of the medical community, alcoholism is a disease because it fits the definition. It has a specific cause. It is certainly a destructive process, progressing inexorably to destruction in those afflicted. As we have seen in earlier chapters it has many characteristic symptoms. The great benefit of the disease model is that secular counselors and physicians now have an entity which can be treated rather than a moral problem which needs to be punished or simply abhorred. From the standpoint of the "helpers" in the secular world, this is invaluable.

Looking at the problem from the other side of the mountain, the Christian comes to a different conclusion. The Bible is very clear that a sin is anything which deviates from the law of God. It tells us the fate of the sinner in general and occasionally prescribes the penalty for perpetrators of particular offenses. The Scripture tells us what to do with a drunkard, or habitual drunk. In the Old Testament, he was to be stoned to death.

DEUTERONOMY 21:21

...and say to the city fathers, "This son of ours is a stubborn rebel; he won't listen to a thing we say. He's a glutton and a drunk." Then all the men of the town are to throw rocks at

---

1   *Journal of the American Medical Association*, **February 1992.**

2   *Webster's New World Dictionary*, **Second College Edition (Simon & Schuster, New York, 1984). Pg. 403.**

him until he's dead. You will have purged the evil pollution
from among you. All Israel will hear what's happened and
be in awe.

(Message Bible)

Under the New Covenant he is in the same class with idolaters, fornicators,
and the like (**1 CORINTHIANS 5:11**).

What I meant was that you are not to associate with
anyone who claims to be a Christian yet indulges in sexual
sin, or is greedy, or worships idols, or is abusive, or a
drunkard, or a swindler. Don't even eat with such people.

(New Living Testament)

It seems pretty clear that God is not all that thrilled with a drunkard.
It is important to remember, however, that a drunkard is not necessarily
an alcoholic. A drunkard is anyone who gets drunk regularly. It is with
drunkenness that God is upset. Drunkenness is a sin for anyone, not just an
alcoholic. Sin is any deviation from the law of God. God has given us a clear
prohibition against drunkenness in **ROMANS 13:13-14**.

We should be decent and true in everything we do so that
everyone can approve of our behavior. Don't participate in
wild parties and getting drunk, or in adultery and immoral
living, or in fighting and jealousy. But let the Lord Jesus
take control of you and don't think of ways to indulge your
evil desires.

(New Living Testament)

Paul tells us that drunkenness is contrary to the nature of the Lord
Jesus Christ and reflects the nature of the old, flesh-dominated man. This is
consistent with the inclusion of drunkenness in the list of manifestations of the
flesh given in **GALATIANS 5:19-21**.

When you follow the desires of your sinful nature, your
lives will produce these evil results: sexual immorality,
impure thoughts, eagerness for lustful pleasure, idolatry,
participation in demonic activities, hostility, quarreling,
jealousy, outbursts of anger, selfish ambitions, division,
the feeling that everyone is wrong except those in your own
little group, envy, drunkenness, wild parties, other kinds of
sin. Let me tell you again, as I have said before, that anyone
living that sort of life will not inherit the Kingdom of God.

(New Living Testament)

Notice that drunkenness is just one in a list of many sins. It is not the worst or the best. It is not unpardonable. It is simply a sin. Note also that drunkenness is not alcoholism. This is an important distinction. There are millions of people who drink to drunkenness who are not alcoholics, yet when they get drunk they are guilty of the sin of drunkenness.

When people get drunk they almost invariably commit other sins. Intoxication is the gateway into all kinds of moral derelictions. This is true of anyone who drinks, not just alcoholics. This is what Paul meant when he wrote:

EPHESIANS 5:18

Don't be drunk with wine, because that will ruin your life.
Instead, let the Holy Spirit fill and control you.

(New Living Testament)

When a young man plies his date with wine, he is not appealing to some suspected alcoholism, but to the moral weakening associated with intoxication in general. Intoxication of any kind submits the will to some substance other than God. The person is temporarily controlled by the chemical. God hates this.

The person who habitually gets drunk is like any other habitual sinner. It so happens that his habit leaves him open to a whole array of associated problems, including addiction, which are extremely harmful. The drunkard needs to be corrected and helped before he destroys himself. This is always the purpose in confronting sinful behavior in other believers. As in **1 CORINTHIANS 5:5** with the man living in sexual perversion, the goal with the drunkard is to keep him from going to hell.

...and cast out this man from the fellowship of the church
and into Satan's hands, to punish him, in the hope that his
soul will be saved when our Lord Jesus Christ returns.

(The Living Bible)

Paul goes on in **1 CORINTHIANS 6:9-10** to let us know that habitual drunkenness will keep us from the blessings of the Kingdom:

Do you not know that the wicked will not inherit the
kingdom of God? Do not be deceived: Neither the sexually
immoral nor idolaters nor adulterers nor male prostitutes
nor homosexual offenders nor thieves nor the greedy nor

drunkards nor slanderers nor swindlers will inherit the kingdom of God.

(New International Version)

Again, the judgment is of the sin of drunkenness committed habitually. The goal is to help the individual so as to keep him out of hell. Notice again. There are drunkards who are not alcoholics. They drink to excess regularly and have not yet shown any of the other symptoms of addiction. They are still able to quit as an act of will. This does not exempt them from the fate of the drunkard. By contrast, there are alcoholics who have quit drinking and are still dealing with the physical, social, emotional, and psychological effects of their addiction. These people are not drunkards.

The alcoholic is unfortunate to have a pet sin which is so obvious to all. Many fornicators manage to sneak around for years without getting caught. I suspect we all fellowship daily with people who occasionally slip back into their covetousness or their gossip. These folks can often have a day or two of backsliding, then repent, and few are the wiser. The alcoholic, on the other hand, usually follows his first drink with another and another and another. As he becomes more inebriated he does remarkably stupid and obnoxious things. He is rarely able to keep his derelictions a secret.

I had a friend whose husband was in that class of "occasional" drunk. Once he started, it was difficult for him to stop. This was not a "two beer" kind of guy. Beer number one triggered the craving, and beer number two was inevitable. He was a Christian and an Elder in his church, a really decent man who loved the Lord. Of course, since he was a Christian he could not possibly be an alcoholic. He was a "new creation." Unfortunately, his alcoholic body and brain didn't know this. When he got under great pressure on the job he would occasionally stop for a beer. One beer led to another, and so would begin a binge, usually ended by some disaster. This is alcoholic drinking though it only occurred once a year.

After one particularly destructive bender during which he wrecked the family auto and suffered humiliation before the people in his church, his wife described the pattern to me. I tried to avoid the theological debate concerning disease and sin. I pointed out that the problem lay in his choice of sins. Many is the gossip who can backslide a little, enjoy a great session of tale-bearing, then ask forgiveness and return to the choir loft with no apparent ill effect. The alcoholic, however, rarely backslides quietly. When he takes a little drink it quickly turns into a big drink, and from there often progresses to a bigger stink. When the alcoholic backslides, he does it publicly and loud.

Let's make this as clear as possible. The Bible condemns drunkenness, and habitual drunkenness in particular. By contrast, drinking is not inherently condemned by the Scripture. I know this may be contrary to your best instincts on the subject. Given the destruction I have seen as a result of drinking, I certainly have a great disdain for the practice. But my disdain does not make it a sin! The Scripture refers repeatedly to drinking wine. Although some would have us believe this refers to a non-fermented form of grape juice, the Bible implies otherwise. Consider **ECCLESIASTES 10:19**.

> *Laughter and bread go together, And wine gives sparkle to life--But it's money that makes the world go around.*

(Message Bible)

This is the common word for wine in the Old Testament. Unless it possessed very different properties from grape juice today, this was good old alcohol-laden, fermented wine. What else could be given to make us merry?

I know this puckers the face of the more religious among us, but it is true nonetheless. Not only is the wine referred to in the Bible of the alcoholic variety, but its effects are even recommended at times. The Psalmist includes it in a list of God's blessings: *"...And wine that maketh glad the heart of man."* (**PSALM 104:15**, King James Version).

When Jesus turned the water into wine at the wedding feast, we hear no moralizing lecture on the evils of alcohol. We do, however, see the term "well drunk" (King James Version) used in reference to the activity of wine-drinking. (**JOHN 2:10**)

> *and said to him, "Everyone serves the best wine first. When people are drunk, the host serves cheap wine. But you have saved the best wine for now."*

(God's Word)

The term is quite specific in its reference to intoxication. The idea is that the usual practice was to serve the good stuff, the kind Jesus made, first so the guests could get a little high, then bring in the cheap wine. Whether you like it or not, Jesus turned out some genuine wine.

Even that old Pharisee, Paul, gave room to maneuver on the subject. When he was giving rules for the selection of leaders in the church he only said they could not be "given to wine." (**1 TIMOTHY 3:3**) They could drink as long as they were not controlled by it. He even suggested to Timothy that a little wine might be good for his digestive difficulties (**1 TIMOTHY 5:23**). I don't know about you, but I have never known grape juice to be recommended in this medicinal manner.

Possibly the most telling passage in the Scripture on the subject is in **PROVERBS 31**. Notice first verses **6 & 7**:

> *Give beer to those who are perishing, wine to those who are in anguish; let them drink and forget their poverty and remember their misery no more.*

(New International Version)

This is clearly extolling the virtue of intoxicating beverages as a temporary aid to those in severe distress. I don't think this is Welch's. While there is certainly room for debate as to how far we can take this principle in actual practice, I think it proves that the Bible is not always condemnatory of drinking.

Before you take up stones, let me address the concept of drinking for a modern American Christian. We live in a society reeling from the effects of alcohol and drug abuse. Lives are being destroyed all around us. In that social context I find it irresponsible for any Christian to do anything which might be construed as permission to drink. That certainly includes example. At the very least, those in positions of Christian leadership ought to be examples of abstinence without fault-finding. I believe this applies to drugs and nicotine as well.

Paul sets out a principle in **ROMANS 14:21-23**.

> *The right thing to do is to keep from eating meat, drinking wine, or doing anything else that will make other believers fall. Keep what you believe about this matter, then, between yourself and God. Happy are those who do not feel guilty when they do something they judge is right! But if they have doubts about what they eat, God condemns them when they eat it, because their action is not based on faith. And anything that is not based on faith is sin.*

(Good News Bible)

Your entry into the kingdom will not be determined by what you eat and drink. By the opposite token, you must control what you eat and drink based on its potential to damage those who see you. I shudder to think some new Christian, a babe in the Lord, would be encouraged to open the door for the return of his alcoholic devils by seeing me partaking of wine with impunity. I am sufficiently serious about this that I do not drink out of containers normally reserved for alcoholic beverages lest someone see me and think I am drinking. Yes, this includes weddings with the traditional toast as well as the popular "non-alcoholic" cocktails and beers.

The flip side of this conviction is that others are free to do what they see fit before God. Unbelievers are under no obligation whatsoever, and their drinking is not nearly as important as their rejection of Christ. I bear them no judgment. For Christians, they may be ignorant or unconvinced. It is my place to live my convictions and let them live theirs. This means that if I am in a restaurant where alcohol is served, I can take my snooty nose down out of the rafters and enjoy my meal without self-reproach or censure of others.

There is another reason the Christian should avoid alcohol and other intoxicants. It deprives him of the privileges of his position in Christ. Notice again **PROVERBS 31:4-5**.

> *"Leaders can't afford to make fools of themselves, gulping wine and swilling beer, Lest, hung over, they don't know right from wrong, and the people who depend on them are hurt.*

(Message Bible)

My Bible tells me clearly that I became royalty when I came to know Christ. I am a king and a priest (**REVELATION 1:6**), a member of a royal priesthood (**1 PETER 2:9**). Therefore it is not for me to partake of strong drink of any kind. This prohibition is not given because God is just a party-pooper. It is given because He loves His children and wants them to be victorious. That means abstaining from anything which might cause me to forget His Word (law) or which might cloud my judgment in dealing with others.

Drunkenness is a sin. It is not the same as alcoholism. It is closely related to alcoholism in two ways. First, it is contributory. Alcoholism is, by definition, caused in part by habitual drunkenness. If you don't drink you will never be an alcoholic. Drunkenness is also one of the symptoms of alcoholism. If someone is drinking regularly even though it seems to be creating problems for him, he may well be an alcoholic. This is not the only symptom of alcoholism, but it is certainly a definitive one. Still, alcoholism includes the entire panorama of emotional, physical, mental, and social problems as well as habitual drunkenness.

The answer to the dilemma is really simple. We have a sin, drunkenness, which causes a disease, alcoholism.

> **_Drunkenness is a sin._**
> **_Alcoholism is a disease._**

This is such an elusive concept we should probably repeat that dyad four or five times:

> _Drunkenness is a sin/Alcoholism is a disease._
>
> _Drunkenness is a sin/Alcoholism is a disease._
>
> _Drunkenness is a sin/Alcoholism is a disease._
>
> _Drunkenness is a sin/Alcoholism is a disease. Etc._

The idea of a disease process which is caused, triggered, or exacerbated by a sinful behavior should be easy to swallow. There are many sins which are involved in a disease. We all know people who knowingly desecrate the Temple of God with cigarette smoke and wind up with emphysema or cancer. Our senses are bombarded daily with news about the relationship of diet to heart disease, yet gluttons continue to plug their arteries.

The largest objection to the idea of alcoholism as a disease is the sense that this designation absolves the alcoholic of responsibility for his behavior. This is just not so. Not if we have a right understanding of a disease. As with any other sin-related disease, the alcoholic is responsible to cooperate in his treatment and modify his sinful behavior to ameliorate the symptoms of the disease. The emphysema patient must stop smoking. The heart patient must amend diet and exercise patterns. It is up to them. So also for the alcoholic. He must seek out and cooperate in appropriate treatment.

I remember when my dad was suffering with emphysema. He had smoked for a lifetime. He was a good, Christian man, but he lived before all the horrors of smoking were known. When the disease began to debilitate his body, we never spent a great deal of time telling him how awful he was because he had caused this terrible condition. No one looked down their nose at him or implied that he deserved to suffer. We simply tried to help him overcome the disabilities associated with emphysema.

As a pastor, I have visited many people in the hospital. Many of them have been very heavy people with heart problems. Even though I am a jogger and watch my diet, I have never had the slightest inclination to lecture these people about their lifestyle. That may come later, but for now I offer prayer and encouragement to hang tough and follow the treatment plan.

Imagine yourself as suffering with pneumonia. Your lungs are full of fluid and your cough shakes you to the depths of your being. You are straining for every breath. Desperate, you go to the emergency room. Doctor #1 greets you with the news that you are horribly wicked. He curses you for exposing yourself to germs, and tells you to stop coughing or you are going to go to hell. Hurt, frightened, and angry you go to another hospital. Doctor #2 tells you that you are suffering with a grave illness, but there is hope. He gives you something for the cough, prescribes some antibiotics to deal with the cause of the infection, and tells the staff to help you with normal activities until you are strong enough to help yourself. Which doctor would you prefer?

The experience of most alcoholics in the church is very much like doctor #1. They come in anguish seeking help and are met with recriminations. Unable to quit drinking, they are condemned as weak-willed and insincere. If they are lucky, they find their way to doctor #2, whether in a treatment center or in Alcoholics Anonymous. They find out they have a disease which is fatal, but there is hope if they will cooperate. They find support to stop the drinking and a framework for dealing with the problems that accompany it. Not surprisingly, most choose doctor #2. Unfortunately Doctor #2 rarely offers help in finding eternal salvation, only temporal relief.

I am going to take the liberty of referring to alcoholism as a disease. If you choose to call it something else, feel free. I am quite comfortable with that designation for addiction to alcohol and all the psychological, physical, and social problems which accompany it. It seems clear to me that removing the alcohol from the alcoholic cures some of these problems in time. Others require more attention. The body is still sensitized to alcohol and will respond addictively to ingestion. The mind is caught in an addictive world view. The emotions are labile from years of being sedated. Social skills are inadequate and social circles are gone. There is a lot of work yet to do.

FAMILY FALLOUT

It is with great fear and trembling that I approach the subject of the home. There has been a great deal of literature generated on the topic. We have coined any number of terms which have been bandied about on T.V. talk shows until we all know the words: Co-dependent, Co-alcoholic, Adult Child of an Alcoholic, and of course, the dreaded Dysfunctional Family. We all know the words, but do they have any real meaning? How do they help us describe the effects of addiction on the family?

The terms co-dependent or co-alcoholic are used to describe those who are in some kind of relationship to an addict, usually a spouse. The definitions are myriad and not a little hazy. The common thread in all of them seems to be that there are destructive effects wrought upon the psychological, emotional, physical, and spiritual conditions of those who love an addict. Because their lives revolve around a person whose existence is in chaos, they are always affected. The idea seems to be that they are dependent on the addict, who is dependent on the drug, and they are therefore "co-dependent." Their destruction proceeds in tandem with the addict's.

The "dysfunctional family" is a bit easier to define. The word "dysfunctional" means anything that doesn't work the way it is supposed to. The family is designed to provide a unit of stability in every culture. It is the place where children are conceived, raised, protected, and provided for. It is where we learn our values and where we go for support in difficult times. It is the unit which nurtures the young and cares for the elderly. It passes along the values and traditions of the larger culture and is the place of primary personal interaction. The alcoholic home does none of these very well. It doesn't work. It is dysfunctional.

> *The word "dysfunctional" means anything that doesn't work the way it is supposed to.*

If the alcoholic family doesn't do what a family is supposed to do, and if the primary purpose of a family is to raise children, then it should come as no surprise that children of alcoholic parents don't turn out according to design. They come to adulthood with a warped view of themselves, of family, and of the world. They enter into the raising of their own families with no information concerning the normal function of a family, and therefore often produce a second generation of dysfunction.

Rather than try to discuss co-dependency or family theory at any length, I want to identify a few commonalities in the experience of people from alcoholic homes. There are rules and roles in every home. The rules and roles in the alcoholic home are set in motion to protect and appease a sick individual. They therefore produce behaviors and attitudes which are adaptive only in a sick environment. The individual who lives out these rules and roles is uncomfortable and ineffective in a healthy, open setting. As we look at some of these, you may see some familiar things. Others may be less so. These are simply some of the things which happen in alcoholic homes which have echoes throughout the lives of the individuals involved.

In the home of the alcoholic/addict, the drug is the organizing principle. Though it may only be mentioned during times of emotional explosion, it is constantly present in the awareness of everyone. It is the important issue of every day. Family members count drinks. They make up activities to keep the alcoholic busy and away from the bottle. They pour liquor down the toilet and search for hidden bottles. Every trip to the store is a cause for alarm. Every welcoming kiss is accompanied by a sniff of the breath. The family concentrates on making supply scarce while the addict is dedicated to guaranteeing its availability. Suspicion is the rule, even in good moments.

Often the family suffers as much from denial as the alcoholic. They buy into his excuses. They sympathize with his "stressful" job and defend him to critical friends. Problems of all sorts may be identified: health, finances, weather, soup and nuts. But rarely is the connection to alcohol recognized. Members of alcoholic families often seek professional help and never mention the drinking in the home. It is so much a part of the day-to-day fabric of life that its place in their personal turmoil is overlooked. It isn't unusual for them to respond with a "no" when questioned about drinking problems in the family.

In the home of the alcoholic/addict, the drug is the organizing principle.

I recall one young woman, a good Christian lady, who was married to an adulterer and drug abuser. He required of her some of the most degrading and vile behaviors imaginable. After years of this treatment, the marriage finally broke up at his behest. She found her way to my office depressed over her sense of failure in the marriage. Her perception of herself was such that if any significant person, especially her husband, was unhappy or unsuccessful, the blame was hers. It took considerable digging before she finally noted that her father was a severe alcoholic who managed to sell this same package to his whole household. His wife and children were responsible for his behavior. She went into marriage a perfect victim for the slaughter, ready to believe she was responsible for the behavior of an addict.

The family of the alcoholic is determined to keep the boat upright at all costs. Don't you dare rock it! The term "walking on eggshells" was coined to describe the addicts household. In times of relative calm, everyone wants desperately to believe that all is well and things will be better now. Anyone who threatens to trouble the waters is quickly corrected by the other clansmen. Peace at any cost. The inevitable return to uproar begins the search for someone

> **"Walking on eggshells"**

to blame. Maybe supper really should have been five minutes later or Junior should have shown more deference. After all, it couldn't be that dad is just a drunk!

Alcoholism is not a pretty disease nor is it socially acceptable. Because the family is ashamed, they usually join together to enable the drunk to avoid the consequences of his behavior. They learn to make up stories at the drop of a hat. Mom calls the boss to report dad's self-induced illness as "the flu." Little Billy takes responsibility to care for his siblings because mom is too drunk. Jimmy tells the police it was he who drove the car into the neighbor's flowers. Money is spent on cleaning up after the drunk rather than the needs of other family members. The unspoken motto is "maintain the family at all costs." Lying is a way of life. Ignoring the obvious allows life to go on.

The most rigorous restriction on family members is "Don't Talk!" This is first directed at outsiders. We don't want anyone to know our shame. We don't make plans or invite people in. We don't know what might happen. When something does happen, we must pretend it didn't. The silence creeps into family relationships. Alliances are formed and dissolved with the shifting sands of the alcoholic's favor or contempt. Expression of any sort of discontent comes under the classification of rocking the boat and is discouraged. People learn to walk through life with their miseries inside. Formation of outside friendships is well-nigh impossible. The normal sources of support and advice are simply unavailable.

Because of the unpredictable nature of the alcoholic, and because his behavior determines every aspect of family life, there is precious little trust in the alcoholic home. It doesn't matter what is planned on a given day, it can all change in an instant. The deceit may range from not getting to go to the ball game to coming home to find the furniture sold at auction. Broken promises are the norm.

It's not just broken promises that cause insecurities in the family of the alcoholic. For the little ones there is the constant experience of being told their perceptions are wrong. Daddy may look drunk. He may act drunk. He may have alcohol on his breath. But your birthday party is canceled because he is sick, not drunk. Don't even think such a thing. Mommy promised you a new dress, but she was blacked out when she said it. She doesn't remember, and she would never lie. Therefore it is you who are wrong. Why would you make up such a story?

> *The greatest gift a family can give a child is the sense of safety and well-being that comes with consistency and stability. The alcoholic home has none of this.*

The greatest gift a family can give a child is the sense of safety and well-being that comes with consistency and stability. The alcoholic home has none of this. Every step must be taken tentatively lest the rug disappear from beneath our feet. Economic difficulties are common to alcoholics. Jobs are lost. Payments are ignored. Lawyers are hired. Addiction is an expensive pastime. Alcohol is a solvent which dissolves relationships. Marriages come and go. The ones that last are either volatile and dangerous or silent and miserable. None of this even addresses the physical and sexual abuses perpetrated in the alcoholic home. It is a dangerous and unpredictable place to live.

All these things leave scars on children. When you grow up in insanity, insanity becomes the norm. It often takes total collapse for the children of such families to get help. Instead, they often seek out families like their own in order to be in a familiar environment. Over half of all alcoholics are children of alcoholics. Sixty percent of the women who marry alcoholics had alcoholic fathers. Everyone

When you grow up in insanity, insanity becomes the norm.

develops ways of thinking and behaving which enable them to survive in their environment.

Psychologists have described several typical personality patterns which people in the alcoholic home develop as a means of coping with their situation. I know the word "psychology" makes some Christians nervous, and I will admit that they have come up with some very bizarre ideas. Psychology, however, is simply the study of the psyche, or the Greek *"psuche."* This is the word we most often translate "soul." Psychologists can give us some insight into behavior patterns associated with the thought processes, the emotions, and the will. The fact that most psychologists have no idea about the spirit nature of man leaves them grasping in the dark for answers, but some of their observations do give us a general idea of how people behave.

The roles in the alcoholic home are often fluid and there will always be some overlap. No one perfectly fits any profile. Since there is no perfect home where everyone lives in absolute love and wisdom at all times, everyone may see some degree of these behaviors in himself. The idea is to identify similarities, recognize problems, and become motivated to seek assistance if needed. With that disclaimer, I want to describe a few of the adaptive roles in the alcoholic home.

The head co-dependent is usually the spouse, although an older child may eventually step into this role as well. This is the **ENABLER**. Someone has to take this role in order for an alcoholic to continue to live in a family setting. This is the person in charge of being strong at all times and covering for the alcoholic. He often elicits much sympathy from friends and relatives for dealing with the situation so courageously. The Enabler keeps the family going by assuming the responsibility of dealing with problems caused by the alcoholic's drinking. Externally strong, this individual often has feelings of great anger, feeling martyred and self-righteous. The Enabler often has difficulty adjusting if the alcoholic sobers up and begins to take his responsibilities seriously.

Another set of adaptive behaviors is often embodied in one of the oldest children. The family with an addict needs someone to cheer for, and someone to accept responsibility for younger children. The alcoholic consumes all the energies of the Enabler producing a need for an ally. This is the designated achiever, or **HERO**. This individual is often quite successful in school, a star athlete or an honor student. He provides the family with some sense of pride, and often gives the alcoholic a reason to believe everything is OK: "See what a great kid Billy is? I must be doing something right." He is usually a tireless worker, constantly striving to receive approval. Inside he is often filled with anger and feelings of inadequacy. He may grow up to be a workaholic married to a dependent person. Mid-life collapse into depression is not uncommon.

Adaptive Roles
Found in the
Alcoholic Home:

Enabler

Hero

The Scape-Goat

The Lost Child

The Family Clown

With the alcoholic in denial, the Enabler busy being strong, and the Hero winning at life, someone must be responsible for the chaos in this house. This job falls to the **SCAPE-GOAT**. Often a middle child, this is the hostile, rebellious kid who gets all the negative attention. He's the one who gets comments like "I had your brother in class. Why can't you be more like him?" This kid is a prime candidate for trouble with the law, dropping out of school, drug problems, or unplanned pregnancies. His internal hurt, guilt and loneliness keep him on the outskirts of family and society. He makes a great person to take the focus off the alcoholic's drinking.

Another popular adaptation to the turmoil of the alcoholic home is simply to hide, to be the **LOST CHILD**. Some children just turn inward and are "missing in action" emotionally. This loner is quiet and withdrawn. He makes few friends and causes no problems. He may be a great relief to his parents because he is "such a quiet child." He may spend hours playing alone and is a prime candidate for "imaginary friends." This kind of adaptation usually hides an internal environment of great loneliness and feelings of separation, a child who feels invisible. A life of difficulty in forming healthy relationships, especially with the opposite sex, is not unusual.

The most likeable role adaptation is the **FAMILY CLOWN**. He provides a source of comic relief to the tensions in the house. This is the compulsively funny, often sarcastic, individual who can't tolerate tension or confrontation. He laughs his way out of everything. His school life is marked by a short attention span or hyperactivity. He is often emotionally fragile and immature. This character frequently looks for a good, high-achieving Hero to marry.

These are only brief sketches of the difficulties which arise in the home of an alcoholic. Over several years of sharing this information in churches, I have found that there are those in every audience who suddenly recognize themselves in some of the descriptions given here. This often provides them with a glimmer of hope that someone may understand how they feel inside and that relief may actually be available. These things are true. It is also true that no one in an alcoholic home escapes unscathed. If you were there, you were affected. If any of it rings a bell with you, I advise that you seek counsel from someone familiar with alcoholic families, or, at the very least, avail yourself of some of the literature available. (See the Appendix)

In the previous chapters we have discussed the nature and extent of the problem. If you are an addict or alcoholic, you have probably recognized yourself. If so you will want to acquire the accompanying workbook *"Seven Principles of Recovery"* for help in overcoming your difficulties. If you are one who is interested in helping the addict, you will find the following chapters helpful as we discuss some of the strategies available.

THEY ARE OUT THERE

Unless you are living in a plastic bubble, you are part of a church that has a drug and alcohol problem. By that I mean that a significant number of people in your church either are addicted, were addicted, or love an addict. The usual numbers tell us that about 1 in every 3 people are personally impacted by alcohol. That doesn't even count illegal drugs. Your church very likely reflects these numbers. On any given Sunday you may rest assured that at least every third person in the pew needs this book.

From the first time I broached the subject from the pulpit I have been continually amazed at the large number of people with a personal tale to tell. I preached the first set of messages on alcoholism shortly after we started our church in Upstate New York. We were still quite small and meeting in a rented room in the American Legion. When the Lord told me to minister on alcohol and drug addiction on Sunday evenings, I argued with Him. Attendance at our Sunday evening service was sparse enough without further limiting their appeal.

Denial extends from the barroom to the bedroom to the board room, and to the pulpit.

As usual with the Lord, He won the debate. I dutifully announced that we would begin a series on alcoholism and drug addiction the next Sunday evening. With precious little conviction, I encouraged people to invite friends and family who had addictive problems, either personally or in their family. Much to my surprise, our Sunday night attendance doubled and continued at that level throughout six weeks of lessons. In addition, the tapes of that series have since been far and away our largest selling set. We have had testimonies from all over the country of people who were helped.

A few years later we put together a one-day seminar to run in the local church. We ran it in our own church, again, with good response. A pastor friend invited us to repeat it in his church, which we did. His comment afterward was instructive: "I had no idea there were so many people affected." That is exactly the problem. Most pastors have no idea. Denial extends from the barroom to the bedroom to the board room, and to the pulpit. People just don't tell us unless they think we might understand.

As a result of our open recognition of the problem and an honest attempt to be helpful we found our congregation growing with people interested in recovery. Our friend's church experienced the same effect. I will warn you now, if you don't want to see hurting people come to your church for help, then don't address this issue. The world and the church are overrun with people who need help and will come looking for you if you claim to have it. They don't want pat religious answers. They are looking for knowledgeable and compassionate responses. This is a huge field white for harvest.

CAN YOU HELP ME?

If an addict reaches a point of desperation sufficient to drive him to seek help, he has three general options. The first is the church. For those raised in church this is a very natural choice. For others, it is a place to which they are referred by loved ones: "Bob, you need to talk to my pastor." It was the first place I went when it was clear I needed help. I found none. The second option is a counselor or treatment facility of some kind. The third alternative is to go directly to Alcoholics Anonymous. Many a drunk has sobered up in those informal meetings. Fortunately, a person can find God through any of these avenues, especially if the church is sensitive to the plight of the pilgrim.

> *When the alcoholic/addict reaches that point of desperation, he has 3 options:*
> - *the church*
> - *a counselor or treatment*
> - *Alcoholics Anonymous*

GO AND SIN NO MORE

When an addict appears at the church door, his experience is usually dependent on the philosophy or theology of that particular group. In some churches we see his condition as entirely a sin problem. We inform him of his need to quit drinking or drugging. We tell him that if he will sincerely repent and put the bottle down, God will forgive him and all will be well. He calls upon the name of the Lord and we declare him to be saved. He feels better having been washed clean of his guilt. He embarks on a few days, weeks, or months of relative calm while learning about this new life in Christ. Most of what he learns may prepare him for a theology quiz, but it rarely prepares him to live sober.

Unfortunately, simply abstaining from the drug does not cure a person from addiction. It does take care of the immediate problems and

> **Simply "not using" does not cure a person from addiction.**

pressures, and in a few days symptoms of physical withdrawal subside. Irate relatives are now overjoyed or at least cautiously optimistic. This does not, however, help him with the mental habits of a lifetime and the emotional immaturity and insecurities which inevitably dog him. Fear, resentment, and selfishness still abide in his inner life and they rear their ugly heads all too quickly. He often drinks again and we declare him to be backslidden or insincere. He has now proven that "the God thing" doesn't work, or that he is simply too weak to work it. Either way, the church no longer holds hope for him.

Sometimes, especially if our pigeon is a very wealthy or talented person, we give him a new addiction to substitute for his alcohol. Being a compulsive, he begins to work in the church day and night. He makes a name for himself as a wonderful man of God. He is soon involved in many ministries and we place him on the Board of Something or Other. He finds his manipulative talents particularly helpful in this spiritual endeavor. Christian people are always eager to believe in a man who is such a miracle. (Churches are a haven for the co-dependents of the world, eagerly waiting for new wastelings to save.) We are ever looking for any warm body to perform needed tasks in the church. How much better if the body is talented, sincere, and charming. ("He's such a nice guy when he's not drinking.")

Again, if there is no real personal growth but only achievement and approval-seeking, a fall is almost inevitable. We find him one day sneaking out of a bar or a bedroom, again living a life of denial and deceit. He has temporarily satiated his addiction with the good feelings that come from being a spiritual star, but he has not dealt with ways of thinking and relating to others which are thoroughly ungodly. In his unconfronted pride, he finds it easy to rationalize wayward behavior. "After all, look at me. I'm the man

> **The natural thing for an alcoholic/addict to do is blame others for their discomfort.**

of God." Guilt prompts his alcoholic mind to scheme instead of repent. The natural thing for him to do is blame others for his discomfort. He can't look to others in the church for help. Why, he's a star! In the church, if we can't cure a compulsive we simply put him in charge.

Before you write me, let me add that I know there are those who seem to be real alcoholics who find Christ and live out their life without drinking again. I praise God for them but find them to be the exception rather than the rule. There are also in this category many who remain free from alcohol, but never seem to develop emotionally. They tend toward theological legalism and personal irascibility. They seem to refrain from drinking because they know they must, but they hate every minute. Their resentment toward those who still drink is manifest in self-righteousness. These are the folks of whom I used to say, "If I have to be like you, I'd rather be drunk."

RISE AND BE HEALED!

If our alcoholic friend happens to find his way to a charismatic congregation, he might have a slightly different experience. While he will certainly be encouraged to repent and be born again, healing prayer may also be offered. In some churches, someone will lay their hands on him and declare him to be healed of his condition. In other venues, someone will yell at him in the Name of Jesus and command those awful old demons of alcoholism and addiction to come out. Often, he will be pronounced healed and delivered and informed he is now free.

This is an unfortunate choice of words. Unless there is a genuine entry into the ongoing process of sanctification and renewing of the mind, there will be no long-term sobriety. The mental, relational, and emotional habits of a lifetime will usually prevail. Two things often happen. First, the desire to drink returns. The reasoning of the alcoholic is simple. If I still want a drink, then I must not be healed and I might as well partake. Second, the alcoholic's remarkably imaginative mind says that a healed person can drink if he so desires. What's a little wine among friends?

> *Unless there is a genuine entry into an ongoing process of recovery, there will be NO long-term sobriety.*

Again, I am well-acquainted with those who come to the altar, get delivered, and live out their lives without drinking. I am thrilled for them. I have prayed for many of them. I have seen God do amazing things instantaneously. It just doesn't happen that way for everybody. To tell people it does is to mislead them and ill-prepare them for the demands of living sober in the real world.

For both types of "instant" sobriety, conversion or healing, there is a higher standard of well-being than simple abstinence. If a person is abstinent but continues to evidence the other problems of alcoholism, then they are dry but not sober. Dry alcoholics tend to live on an emotional roller coaster, careening from elation to depression, even going so far as to be diagnosed with manic-depressive disorders. They may have difficulty in forming relationships with deep personal attachments. They may be bitter and judgmental. Fear may prompt hoarding and defensiveness. Their family may say they liked them better when they were drinking.

We often help them in their maladaptation by giving them spiritual license for their sinful attitudes. The defense mechanisms which served them as drunks are now magically sanctified into assets. Denial is now faith. If I admit a problem I am showing a lack of faith, therefore I deny the existence of my fears, resentment, and self-centeredness. Projection is now prophetic insight. Displacement is now righteous indignation. Rationalization becomes revelation. An obsessive preoccupation with religious rites and duties takes the place of a love affair with a chemical. Obsession is now masked as consecration. This is not freedom, but illusion and bondage.

I believe strongly in the power of repentance and in the need for healing and deliverance. In the early days of my ministry I had few opportunities to preach so I often went to the unsavory sections of town to pass out tracts and pray for people as the opportunity arose. One frigid winter morning I went with some companions to the area near the rescue mission in Oklahoma City. There, in the middle of an empty lot, we found three very drunk individuals lying on the ground. They were all heavily bundled in old parkas which smelled strongly of urine, sweat, and stale Mogen David.

When we approached them with an offer of a tract and prayer, one fellow cursed us. Another of them, however, expressed an interest. This one turned out to be a woman, recognizable as such only because she told us. They related that they had been turned away from the mission because of their repeated rule violations. We eventually prayed for the woman and her husband while their companion continued to curse. They made a profession of faith in Christ and we prayed for them to receive the Holy Spirit. Both spoke with tongues and the woman began to give a beautiful prophecy about the soon return of the Lord. They were struck sober. The family was healed and at last report they were working in the mission. God does miracles in the Name of Jesus.

In my own case, I know I was demonized. The first night I spent in my apartment sober and without sedation I saw the face of my devil. He looked like a small black dog with awful, snarling teeth and red-ingot eyes. He would spring out of the darkness onto my bed, prompting me to leap up screaming. It was a long night. I finally left all the lights on. He didn't seem to like the light. For four months I stayed sober on desire and the support of other people. I wanted a drink every hour of every day. Something inside of me drove me toward it with a pressure that is indescribable to the normal person.

At the end of four months, I knew I could no longer resist the drive within me. It was exactly that, an inner drive. Psychologically, it manifested itself in a sense of unreality about the world around me. I felt as if other people existed on the other side of an invisible shield. I wanted to scream and pound on the window to get their attention, to become a part of the rest of the world. I finally fell to my knees and cried out to God, beseeching His help with the sincerity only desperation can muster. I immediately felt something physically lift off my body. The shield was gone and something I can only describe as darkness left me. From that point forward all temptations to drink or use drugs were thoughts which came at my mind from the outside. The drive in my belly was gone.

Both these instances illustrate the delivering power of God. They also indicate two of the many different ways in which that power may come to bear on the distress of an individual. It is a mistake to prepare a formula based on the experience of any one person or group. God did the work in each instance in a way specific to His knowledge of the person involved. The factor that spelled success in both cases was the availability of Christian people to help in the process of discipleship. She went to

Success is possible when Christians are willing and available to walk side by side the alcoholic until that person can walk alone.

the city rescue mission. I went to a support group where I found a number of Christian people who walked side by side with me until I could walk alone. The process was not easy and was fraught with dangers.

I must admit to a certain irritation with God over these differences in individual experience. When I realized I had to quit smoking cigarettes I was already a Christian. I knew something about the Word of God and the power of God to deliver. I prayed, I praised, I confessed my deliverance. Still, I went through several days of fairly intense withdrawals, complete with sleeplessness, headaches, irritability, and the like. Thank God for His grace which brought me through. On the other hand, I know many people who came up in a prayer line and were instantaneously freed from any desire to smoke. I was befuddled as to why some get it immediately, and seemingly painlessly, while others have to endure great discomfort.

> *Obeying the Word of God when it doesn't feel good causes that Word to cut away the dead places and restore our hearts to sensitivity.*

As I continued in ministry I saw more instances of this phenomenon. I actually began to believe that God might be a respecter of persons. He apparently simply liked some better than others. I bothered Him about this fairly regularly. Finally, He saw fit to help me with my question. One day as I watched a popular Christian talk show I heard a story which gave me the key to the problem.

The guest was a dear lady who gave a rather lengthy testimony of alcohol and drug abuse. She related three episodes of addiction. After youthful indiscretions led to drug problems, she came to church, came to the altar, and was instantly saved and delivered. She married a Christian man and did well for a while. Later she sank back into addiction. After an appropriately miserable period, she returned to the church, returned to the altar, received prayer, and was again instantly delivered from the desire for drugs. Again came a marriage, a backsliding, a period of misery, and a return to the altar.

On this third trip to the prayer rail she fully expected to receive the same results. This time, however, despite sincere repentance, she received no symptomatic relief from her addiction. Because she was sincere in her desire to serve the Lord, she continued drug-free but endured a daily struggle with the desire to use. Fear and confusion assaulted her mind. She earnestly asked God why she was still in this plight. According to her testimony, God spoke to her heart saying, "You walked away. You walk back."

Now this may not suit your theology, but it really helped me. I began to ask questions of those to whom I ministered. A pattern seemed evident. It is easier for non-Christians and nominal Christians to get free than for those who have been genuinely born again. The Lord reminded me of what Paul wrote to Timothy about seared consciences:

1 TIMOTHY 4:2

These liars have lied so well and for so long that they've lost their capacity for truth.

(Message Bible)

I have come to believe that those who know God and still walk into drug or alcohol abuse, cause their consciences to become callous. There is a hardness of heart that comes with knowingly doing wrong. In order to remove this spiritual scar tissue the Lord sometimes requires us to walk according to His Word by sheer faith, with no feelings to encourage us. As children of God, we have a reborn heart. We do not need to be born again, again. We need to have the scar tissue surgically removed. This is done using the sword of the Spirit. Obeying the Word of God when it doesn't feel good causes that Word to cut away the dead places and restore our hearts to sensitivity. This may take time.

I was saved in the Southern Baptist Church when I was fourteen. The whole time I was using and drinking I knew I was wrong. My heart told me so. Every time I ignored my conscience my reborn heart became a little harder. It was necessary for God to use terribly adverse circumstances to drive me back to Himself. This is often the case of the backslider. God never forgets our commitments to Him. He promises to correct His children. When we resist Him to the point that our heart becomes callous, He intervenes by allowing circumstances to correct us. In many cases this brings us to the place of obedience and allows the Word to do heart surgery. The Christian makes a poor sinner. We just can't keep it up as long as the unbeliever. God won't allow it.

The unbeliever, on the other hand, has a heart which is wicked by nature. While he may have some vague sense of right and wrong, he feels no obligation to do the right thing. God is under no obligation to correct his behavior. When the unbeliever approaches God, he needs a complete heart transplant. When he calls on the Name of the Lord he is born again and receives a new heart with a clean slate. If he then proceeds into real discipleship, he can live free. These are the people who receive instant deliverance.

When an addict turns to the church for help, he needs all we have to offer. If he is an unbeliever, he obviously needs to be saved. Sobriety won't get you into heaven. If he is bound by demonic forces, he needs to be delivered. He certainly needs prayer for the healing of his body and mind. Having done all that, he also needs a structured program of discipleship which will help him avoid the pitfalls inherent in his addictive past while he learns to walk with the Lord. It helps if he has someone who is familiar with the peculiar thinking of the addict to help him as he goes.

SEE THE YELLOW PAGES UNDER "ALCOHOLISM"

The secular world has many options for the alcoholic in search of treatment. Nearly every hospital now has a special unit for addictions. There are ads in the newspaper, commercials on television, and a whole section in the Yellow Pages. There are both inpatient and outpatient services. The usual inpatient program requires about a 4-week hospitalization with at least a year of outpatient follow-up. Costs are widely variable and may be covered by insurance. Outpatient services range from weekly counseling to day-care settings. While I feel the inpatient setting is preferable, there are those who can and do stay sober in an outpatient program. Physical condition and financial reality play a part in this decision.

The biggest barrier to recovery for the alcoholic: denial of his condition.

The first responsibility of the treatment facility is to assess the physical needs of the addict. Withdrawal from alcohol can be life threatening. Detoxification in a medically supervised setting may be indicated. In addition, alcohol causes secondary physical problems which may be aggravated by withdrawals or which may need immediate attention in their own right. I would encourage every alcoholic to see a physician for help in the withdrawal process. The same is true for addiction to other drugs. Each one has its peculiar problems which need the attention of those who are expert in the field.

During the detoxification period there begins the second function of the treatment center: education. From the moment he is able to understand information, the addict needs to be bombarded with the facts of his condition. The biggest barrier to recovery for the addict is denial of his condition. He has an amazing ability to forget his distress. Entry into treatment is a great time to help him see the correlation between his behavior and the symptoms of alcoholism and addiction. The more information he gets about his disease, the more likely he is to recognize it in himself. This is not the time for sympathy, but for reality. He needs to experience his misery as the consequences of his addiction.

As his treatment progresses, he may have to be confronted very directly with the destruction wrought by his behavior, both to himself and those whom he claims to care for. This can be a very

> *The death of DENIAL is a painful process, but it must happen for recovery to begin.*

uncomfortable process. During this time the alcoholic will probably attempt to convince his family that he is being mistreated and should go home post haste. It is important for the family to be strong.

There must come a moment when the alcoholic recognizes the gravity of his state and begins to take responsibility for himself. This will never happen as long as there is anyone willing to bail him out.

When denial begins to crack, it may be possible to deal with some of the problems of daily living which confront the addict. This is not the time for in-depth psychotherapy, but he will need to be convinced of the absolute necessity of aftercare. This preparation for discharge should include some family planning sessions. There may be an opportunity for the airing of the worst interpersonal grievances and the beginning of healing in the home. At the very least, the family should receive some education on the nature of addiction and the necessity of continued treatment.

Let me digress momentarily to discuss the differences in treatment centers. First, fancy is not better. The quality of the program and the expertise of the personnel are much more important than the skill of the decorator. Second, be aware that there are widely differing treatment philosophies available in the land. Some centers insist on support groups for aftercare. Others are still convinced that psychological therapy is the best method.

Most centers are now strongly recommending abstinence from alcohol and other drugs. Others are determined that some alcoholics can learn to control their drinking. Some are still prescribing drugs to cause adverse reactions to alcohol.

If you are looking for a treatment program please take time to ask questions. Talk to someone in authority. Ask for the director or a supervisor. Don't talk to the unit clerk about treatment philosophy. Here are some characteristics to look for:

> *1. A commitment to drug-free detoxification, if at all possible.*
>
> *2. Total abstinence from drugs and alcohol as a goal of treatment.*
>
> *3. Availability of 24-hour medical attention.*
>
> *4. A daily schedule which is busy with constructive activities. These should include education meetings, group sessions, and individual counseling. Some recreational activities are desirable, but arts and crafts shops will not keep a person sober. The focus of every minute of every day needs to be recovery.*
>
> *5. Alcoholics Anonymous involvement. This means mandatory attendance at a minimum of two meetings per week. Whether you like it or not, it works.*
>
> *6. A commitment to family involvement in recovery. This means actually bringing the family in for groups and family sessions. An introduction to Alanon is desirable.*
>
> *7. Availability of a Chaplain who at least professes to be a Christian. Most treatment centers give lip service to the spiritual aspect of recovery. The presence of a Chaplain means they have made a commitment of time and resources.*
>
> *8. A staff composed of a mixture of recovering addicts and those with no history of drug or alcohol abuse.*

The vast majority of treatment centers now have one thing in common: they recommend involvement in Alcoholics Anonymous as part of an ongoing program of recovery after discharge. That brings us to the third option for the person seeking help for his alcoholism: A.A.

Don't be afraid of A.A.!

Alcoholics Anonymous is available to anyone free of charge all across the nation. This fact alone makes it a powerful force in helping a person stay sober. Since the mid-1930's millions have been helped through the efforts of A.A. This is a non-professional fellowship of alcoholics who are committed to abstinence as a way of life and look to one another for support in this lifestyle. The experience of many in this fellowship proves that sobriety through A.A. is possible.

The mention of Alcoholics Anonymous evokes a variety of reactions in the Christian community. Some see it as unnecessary. After all, isn't Jesus enough? Others actually believe it to be a cult because of the spiritual emphasis in many of the steps. My contention is that it is a reality whether we like it or not. Most alcoholics are being referred to A.A. either by the courts, by their treatment programs, or by the press of life's circumstances. A.A. is informing them by the tens of thousands every day that they have a disease which requires a spiritual solution. They are encouraged from the beginning to get to know God. This is a prime opportunity for the church to be a blessing, stepping in to fill a spiritual void in the lives of millions of people. In order to be the maximum blessing we need accurate information, not prejudice. The next chapter is devoted to learning about Alcoholics Anonymous.

WHAT ABOUT A.A.?

The current reality of treatment for alcoholism and addiction is that most folks who seek help wind up in Alcoholics Anonymous, or some other twelve step program, for some period of time. To the thousands who have found help there, A.A. has achieved almost sacred status. The fruits are sufficiently obvious to others that there has been a proliferation of other twelve step support groups for every conceivable condition. For the sake of simplicity, we will look at A.A. as the prototype of all its offspring. The group attracts people in need of help. There is practical advice, non-judgmental acceptance, and stories which sound familiar. This is not a bad combination.

One of the basic tenets of Alcoholics Anonymous is the urgency of attending lots of meetings. The most prevalent formula is "90 meetings in 90 days." Most regions have enough meetings available to make this possible. Newcomers who decide they are alcoholic

> *Formula*
> *for a newcomer*
> *to A.A.:*
> *"90 meetings*
> *in 90 days"*

and want to be part of A.A. are told that to do less than "ninety and ninety" is to tempt fate. A.A. and the way of life it teaches are necessary to sobriety, and for the alcoholic to drink is to die. They are told things such as, "You drank every day. You need a meeting every day."

This same message is transmitted to patients in most treatment centers. The majority of treatment facilities start from the first day telling their clients that A.A. involvement is a necessity of recovery. They are rigorously schooled in the hopelessness of alcoholism and the absolute necessity of staying sober. They are informed repeatedly that the best way to stay sober is to go to lots of meetings. The usual line is something like, "If you ask most of those who get drunk what happened to them, they will tell you they quit going to meetings." Attendance in Alcoholics Anonymous meetings is frequently likened to insulin injections for the diabetic. It is necessary for life. The church needs to understand at least two things about this phenomenon. First, the availability of daily support and encouragement is very important to the newly sober alcoholic. "Ninety and ninety" is a good idea. Second, most A.A. people see the program as necessary to their very life. If we tell them they must leave it in order to be Christian, in their mind we may be asking them to choose death. A.A. has some characteristics which will eventually raise questions for the committed Christian. An informed clergy can help the A.A. member grow in Christ until he can make intelligent choices for himself.

"GOD, AS YOU UNDERSTAND HIM?"

Alcoholics Anonymous had its official beginnings in the 1930's. The original A.A. was a New York stockbroker named Bill Wilson. When you see bumper stickers or signs in hotels referring to "friends of Bill W." you have found a place of contact for A.A. members. Wilson was clearly an intelligent and motivated man. He was exposed to the concept of alcoholism as a disease while under treatment with Dr. William Silkworth. The disease concept, coupled with the spiritual influences in his life-form the basis of Alcoholics Anonymous.

Wilson had a conversion experience with Christ in a New York church several months before he actually managed to stay sober. He relates a rather startling encounter with the Lord followed by a brief time of sobriety during a revival under the ministry of Dr. Sam Shoemaker. He became involved in the Oxford Group movement, an offshoot of the Washingtonian Societies which were in turn spawned from Wesley's Methodism.

The disease concept, coupled with the spiritual influences in the life of Dr. William Silkworth, form the basis of Alcoholics Anonymous.

The Oxford Groups were committed to evangelism and spiritual growth. Their program of spiritual growth included a strong commitment to small group ministry, lay ministers, along with daily prayer and journaling. These threads of influence are clearly reflected in A.A. doctrine and practice today. The Oxford Groups also promulgated what they referred to as the four Absolutes of spiritual development: absolute unselfishness, absolute honesty, absolute purity, and absolute love. Again, the echoes of these principles can be heard throughout A.A. literature, including the famous twelve steps.

The Oxford Groups at Calvary Mission in New York had considerable success in converting drunks. Keeping them sober was the problem. It was eventually decided that they may need special groups specifically for them. I'm sure this was a relief to all concerned. Wilson experienced all this, then drank again and returned to Dr. Silkworth's treatment facility, but only after receiving a visit from an old friend who had achieved sobriety under the influence of Dr. Carl Jung, a renowned psychiatrist who believed in spiritual conversion as treatment for alcoholism. During that hospitalization Wilson had another experience with God. In the book "Alcoholics Anonymous," Wilson recounts his desperate cry to God and the response he experienced:

> *"There I humbly offered myself to God, as I then understood Him, to do with me as He would. I placed myself unreservedly under His care and direction. I admitted for the first time that of myself I was nothing; that without Him I was lost. I ruthlessly faced my sins and became willing to have my new-found Friend take them away, root and branch. I have not had a drink since.... We made a list of people I had hurt or toward whom I felt resentment. I expressed my entire willingness to approach these individuals, admitting my wrong. Never was I to be critical of them. ...I was to test my thinking by the new God-consciousness within. Common sense would then become uncommon sense...the effect was electric. There was a sense of victory, followed by such a peace and serenity as I had never known. There was utter confidence. I felt lifted up, as though the great clean wind of a mountain top blew through and through. God comes to most men gradually, but His impact on me was sudden and profound."[1]*

After his discharge from the hospital, he continued an involvement with the Oxford Groups. He became increasingly convinced that helping other drunks was a key to staying sober. As he continued attempting to grow along spiritual lines, he began to accumulate a small group of men who were staying sober. As the movement grew, new ideas were constantly tried and

---

1   *Alcoholics Anonymous*, **Third Edition (Alcoholics Anonymous World Services, Inc, New York City, 1976). Pp. 13-14.**

either kept or discarded depending on their effectiveness. It eventually fell to Bill Wilson to put the common wisdom of the groups into writing in order to more effectively share what they had discovered. This work became the book "Alcoholics Anonymous" or, as it is more commonly known, *"The Big Book."*

> *Bill Wilson never intended A.A. to be an end to a man's spiritual journey, but a beginning. He called A.A. a "spiritual kindergarten."*

The first drafts of the book, and especially the Twelve Steps, were significantly more evangelical in their language than today's version. The reaction from some of the less religiously conservative in the movement caused them to rethink their purpose. It was decided that the program was clearly spiritual, but the primary focus was toward sobriety, not theology. The term "God" would be used with the qualifying phrase "as we understood Him" added to allow for a diversity of theological backgrounds and viewpoints. While some felt the organization, as yet unnamed, should be unabashedly Christian, the general consensus was that the group was designed to help people get sober. They would be encouraged through the program to establish a relationship with God, and the details of that relationship would be up to the individual.

As you can see from this brief history, the roots of Alcoholics Anonymous are decidedly Christian. The early editions of the Big Book included personal testimonies which unabashedly credited Jesus Christ with salvation and sobriety. Bill Wilson never intended the group to be an end to a man's spiritual journey, but a beginning. He called A.A. a "spiritual kindergarten." The official position of the organization has never changed. Alcoholics Anonymous is primarily dedicated to helping alcoholics get sober. Though it encourages spiritual growth through the steps, a person's religion is a personal matter. In the early years, most of those who stayed sober were Christians of one type or another. Bible quotation, and even Bible reading was not uncommon in meetings. However, A.A. has changed just as our society has changed.

The people coming into A.A. meetings are a cross-section of the society at large. They reflect the spiritual beliefs of the community. As our country has strayed from God, so has A.A. In most meetings God is a popular topic. The "as we understand Him" phrase has taken on some most interesting nuances, giving great latitude for the acceptance of very strange ideas. Beginning in the late seventies, treatment centers gained popularity as the "in" way to sober up. The treatment industry is sending graduates into the A.A. community at a remarkable rate. Issues of spirituality are addressed in most treatment centers, but with a decidedly "New Age" bent.

Treatment centers are operated by people trained in psychology, not theology. As a result, the clients get thorough indoctrination in popular mysticism. Many centers actually teach meditation and visualization. Nearly all emphasize the freedom of man to create his own idea of God. Most emphasize the notion that we are all children of God or that God lives in all of us. There is a clear bias toward universalism or Eastern mysticism. As a result, modern A.A. meetings often have a "pop" psychology flavor with a liberal salting of transcendental meditation. This is where the church must be at attention to be of maximum blessing to those involved.

At this juncture I would encourage you to take a careful look at the Twelve Steps of Alcoholics Anonymous.

As you read these Twelve Steps, ask yourself this question: If I understand God to be Jesus Christ, the God of the Bible, do I have any real problem with these steps?

The Twelve Steps of Alcoholics Anonymous[1]

1. We admitted that we were powerless over alcohol – that our lives had become unmanageable.

2. Came to believe that a Power greater than ourselves could restore us to sanity.

3. Made a decision to turn our will and our lives over to the care of God as we understood Him.

4. Made a searching and fearless moral inventory of ourselves.

5. Admitted to God, to ourselves, and to another human being the exact nature of our wrongs.

6. Became entirely ready to have God remove all these defects of character.

---

1   *Alcoholics Anonymous*, Third Edition (Alcoholics Anonymous World Services, Inc, New York City, 1976), pp. 59-60.

7. Humbly asked Him to remove our shortcomings.

8. Made a list of all persons we had harmed and became willing to make amends to them all.

9. Made direct amends to such people whenever possible, except when to do so would injure them or others.

10. Continued to take personal inventory and when we were wrong promptly admitted it.

11. Sought through prayer and meditation to improve our conscious contact with God as we understood Him, praying only for the knowledge of His will for us and the power to carry that out.

12. Having had a spiritual awakening as the result of these steps, we tried to carry this message to alcoholics, and to practice these principles in all our affairs.

In describing the writing of these steps, Bill Wilson gives much credit to God for helping him expand and modify the Four Absolutes of the Oxford Groups. Experience taught the early A.A. pioneers the importance of personal inventory, confession, and restitution in keeping a person sober. They had also discovered the absolute necessity of working to help others. In a truly remarkable insight, the steps are presented in the Big Book as "suggestions" rather than requirements. This is a purposeful recognition of the rebellious character of the alcoholic. All these considerations superseded any theological or doctrinal agenda in the formal writing of the program. The idea is that Christian, Jew, Muslim, or agnostic, all who desire to stay sober could find help in the fellowship of Alcoholics Anonymous.

There can be no doubt that A.A. has provided a life-line for many alcoholics. It has also served as a door into the Kingdom of God for many a lost soul, as well as a signpost on the road home for many who had wandered away from their Christian roots. The organization has a very positive connotation in my mind because of the help I received there. Due to some of the changes in our society and their effects on the average A.A. meeting, there are some problems which must be addressed clearly if we are to help those in our churches who are in A.A. or need to be. AA itself is neither Christian nor non-Christian. It is simply a program of sobriety. The spiritual part of the program is entirely determined by the beliefs and experiences of those in each individual meeting room.

GETTING SOBER, NOT HOLY

When I first entered the Alcoholics Anonymous program I was not very sophisticated in the things of God. As a matter of fact, I didn't know anything. My youthful experiences in the Baptist church had long since been drowned in a flood of alcohol. I thought the mentions of God in the Twelve Steps were a little suspicious. I surely didn't come here to get religion.

My concerns were confirmed when my first sponsor informed me that my initial goal should be to establish a personal relationship with God as I understood him. I was leery of this spiritual talk, but I was also desperate. My attempts were pretty pathetic, but they were flavored with the ardor spawned by extreme circumstances. Not knowing how to pray, I cried out "To whom it may concern." True to His promise, God answered this honest seeker by allowing me to find. I renewed my acquaintance with Jesus.

Many A.A. folk profess and live a spiritual life centered in the fellowship of Alcoholics Anonymous. They claim meetings as their church and the nonthreatening "Higher Power" as their God. I believe that God, in His mercy, winks at these child-like posturings for a season. I was blessed to find people in Alcoholics Anonymous who helped me to move on in my walk with God, progressing from the simple desire to stay sober to a genuine desire to know God.

My second sponsor gave me a great piece of advice. He told me that I came to A.A. to get sober, not holy. His argument was simple and it made sense. If I were to get up in the morning and find that my car wouldn't start, I would need a mechanic, not an A.A. meeting. If I need legal advice I should call a lawyer, not a drunk. Why then, when I want to know God do I expect great theological insight from someone in recovery? Just because people come to A.A. they are not expert in other areas of life. If I want to know God, I need to look beyond the discussions of a room full of

> *My second sponsor gave me a great piece of advice when he told me that I came to A.A. to get sober, not holy!*

alcoholics in various stages of getting well. I need to find someone who knew God and the Bible. Thank God for that wisdom.

When the alcoholic comes into A.A. he is usually a spiritual illiterate. In the meetings he will be directed to get to know God. Unfortunately, he will find precious little knowledge of God there. That is where we come in. With just a little sensitivity to the mind-set of the addict, along with a little knowledge about A.A. and the recovery process, we can help him get in touch with the true and living God and move on with his life. As he grows in the Lord, we can help him get past the things which are inevitable problems for the Christian in A.A.

THIS AIN'T NO CHURCH

Alcoholics Anonymous is not a Christian organization. This is important to remember as we realistically assess what to expect from the group. While they talk at length about "God," there is no pretense that this is the God of the Bible. As a matter of fact, most meetings are liberally sprinkled with those who actively oppose the Word of God. This is to be expected in a group which opens its membership to anyone who has a desire to stop drinking. We should not be surprised at this, nor should we be judgmental of it. This openness to anything or anybody makes for a theological mix which can be quite bizarre. We will discuss that shortly. This also leads to a gamut of behaviors which may be troublesome to a Christian.

If you are an observer entering a meeting for the first time, two things will let you know you are not in church. First, unless expressly prohibited, the majority of people will probably smoke. Second, the conversation will be laced with colorful language, often quite distasteful to the Christian's sensibilities. Both these things are to be expected. Remember where you are. These are largely people from the tavern and cocktail culture. Cursing, smoking, and moral dereliction are a part of daily life. None of them are there because they suddenly decided to become good people. They are universally there because circumstance has forced them to do something about their drinking.

Another clue as to the nature of your surroundings will be the reaction to the Name of Jesus. I have never ceased to marvel at the hostile responses to anyone who gets "too religious." This usually means any expression of a real faith in Christ as evidenced by the usual jargon of the evangelical. A simple "thank You, Jesus" or a "praise the Lord" is likely to be met with silent disdain or overt correction. Even more remarkable is the enthusiasm with which other religions, no matter how bizarre, are embraced. I heard one man say with great seriousness that he prayed to a committee composed of Buddha, Mohammed, Jesus, Abraham Lincoln, and several other luminaries. He asked them to vote and let him know their consensus. My initial response was to stifle a belly laugh. Then I noticed that everyone else was taking him quite seriously.

More than once I have heard comments to the effect that the mention of the Name of Jesus causes very adverse reactions in some A.A. members. Some report that it makes them uncomfortable, a little nervous. Others say it makes them angry. A few even testify to the hair on their neck standing to attention. I have never heard of anyone reacting to other religious figures so violently. Only Jesus is a threat to the demons which befuddle the unbeliever. This has always been a testimony to me of the power that is in the Name of Jesus. There really is "something about that Name."

> *Remember where you are. You are in a room full of people whose common denominator is they are addicted to a chemical.*

Again, rather than get upset and stomp out or declare that A.A. is of the devil, remember where you are. You are in a room full of people whose common denominator is they are addicted to a chemical. They come from mental hospitals, jails, courtrooms, taverns, and side streets. They are thrown together in a room, demons and all. What do you expect? The miracle is that some who are there will sincerely cry out to God and He will meet them where they are.

Because of these behavioral aberrations, it is not uncommon for the A.A. member who becomes a committed Christian to go through some difficult times. He usually begins by trying to share his new-found Savior with his A.A. buddies. Their response is often less than positive. They often tell him he has gotten too religious and needs to be careful lest he drink again. He may find himself being openly castigated in meetings. This can be quite distressing to one who has depended on these gatherings for support, validation, and fellowship. We can often help by simply pointing out to them that their friends are drunks, not Christians, and they are there to get sober, not holy. The price of sharing Christ in this environment is almost sure to be persecution. This places them in the quality company of the saints through the ages.

During my second year in Bible school my wife and I took a short vacation in the beautiful Ozark mountains. The occasion was an A.A. convention. We had been so immersed in church that we had missed our previous involvement in A.A. and we looked forward to a time of rest, encouragement, and fellowship. At the convention we met a couple who had been very important to us in our early sobriety. They were well-known for their work with young people and often spoke in conventions and workshops. As we renewed acquaintance, they inquired about our current business. When we told them they became very angry. We were branded as ungrateful and traitorous. The assault was vicious and painful. The lesson was learned: Some lovely A.A. people will not appreciate our love for Jesus.

After his initial evangelistic zeal is tempered by the realities of A.A. life, the new Christian in A.A. may begin to question his own involvement in the group. He will quite likely begin to feel that he is now too spiritual to need such a carnal association. He may even view it as a hindrance to his Christian life. This presents the pastor or spiritual mentor with a dilemma. The recovering person may actually be ready to stay sober without A.A. It could be that God is leading him out of the support group and into a deeper Christian walk. It could also be that he is looking for an excuse to avoid doing the steps which require him to confront his own behavior and addictive thinking. Whether we like it or not, fervent church work can be a substitute for spiritual and emotional growth.

My wife's sponsor responded with great wisdom to Judy's intention to become active in church. She said, "Just be as involved in the church as you have been in A.A. and you will be all right. The idea of both is to seek God with all your heart." I think this is good advice. Don't let a person who has been attending six A.A. meetings every week suddenly stop and substitute one Sunday morning service. It won't work. They need to become immersed in the things of God, including opportunities for service and socialization.

The Big Book admonishes the recovering alcoholic to, "Be quick to see where religious people are right."

Another good indicator of a person's readiness to cut back on A.A. involvement is his progress in the Twelve Steps. Of particular importance are steps four and five. These steps require the individual to look closely at himself, his behaviors and his attitudes. They also require that he discuss his sinfulness with another human being. I have found this process invaluable to the recovery of addicts. They are so adept at fooling themselves and denying their own responsibility for their lives that without such a review they often cling to old ideas and attitudes to the detriment of themselves and those they love. If you have a friend who wants to quit his A.A. involvement, consider encouraging him to continue attending meetings until he has completed his fourth step and taken his fifth step with someone recommended by his pastor.

Some people are like me. They know they can stay sober and follow God by participation in the church, but they still want to go to an A.A. meeting on occasion. They may want to maintain attendance at their favorite group. Unfortunately they feel uncomfortable in the knowledge that their faith is suspect to their old chums. For these I suggest they simply learn to quote the Big Book. Most A.A.'s will acquiesce when provided with chapter and verse for any behavior. The Big Book admonishes the recovering alcoholic to, "Be quick to see where religious people are right. Make use of what they offer.... Alcoholics who have derided religious people will be helped by such contacts. Being possessed of a spiritual experience, the alcoholic will find he has much in common with these people...he will make new friends and is sure to find new avenues of usefulness and pleasure."[1]

IS GOD REALLY A LIGHT BULB?

As previously mentioned, Alcoholics Anonymous has an interesting array of theologies. In any given meeting all manner of religious backgrounds are represented. Most are very poorly grounded in whatever formal religion they may have come from. The vast majority of the theological notions come from word of mouth picked up in meetings, popular self-help books, and leftovers from the psycho-babble practiced in treatment centers. This provides an eclecticism which is certainly interesting for the observer, but can be quite confusing to the neophyte who is trying to stay sober while sorting out his own Christian beliefs.

---

1   *Alcoholics Anonymous*, **Third Edition (Alcoholics Anonymous World Services, Inc, New York City, 1976), pp. 87,131-132**

The first thing most meetings proclaim is the "God as you understand Him" doctrine. To most people this means that it doesn't matter what you believe about God as long as you believe something. One common inference from this idea is that we can pray to anybody or anything as long as we pray. New members are often told to pray to a light bulb or a door knob. This seems very strange to those who have a personal awareness of a personal Jesus, but it seems to make a great deal of sense to many new drunks.

It would be very easy to get self-righteous about this practice and denounce this evil organization, but there is a more subtle point we need to observe. Jesus promised us that those who seek Him will find Him.

MATTHEW 7:7,8

"Ask, and you will receive. Search, and you will find. Knock, and the door will be opened for you. Everyone who asks will receive. The one who searches will find, and for the one who knocks, the door will be opened."

(God's Word)

"Don't bargain with God. Be direct. Ask for what you need. This isn't a cat-and-mouse, hide-and-seek game we're in."

(Message Bible)

I believe that He is as good as His promise. While the vast majority of people come to A.A. to escape the bitter harvest of their aberrant behavior, some are broken enough to sincerely want to find God. For those who are serious, God is faithful. He finds a way to introduce them to Himself. Whether they begin by calling out to a door knob or by grudgingly talking to a childhood Sunday School memory, God finds the cracks of sincerity through which to shine His healing light.

Somewhat less benign is the philosophy which takes "God as you understand Him" to mean that we can fashion God to suit our understanding. I have often heard the phrase, "Make your God however you want Him to be." I can almost hear the cringing in my formally trained Christian brethren as they read this. It leads to exactly what you might expect: God is cast in a form which suits the tastes and weaknesses of people. It places men in the position of creating God in their image. This thinking has opened the door to all manner of New Age concepts.

In order to assist people in navigating these treacherous theological waters, it is again necessary to make them aware of the differences between Christian theology and the pop-psychology they are likely to hear in A.A. meetings. If they can be encouraged to derive their beliefs from the Bible rather than from the opinions of alcoholics they will not have too much trouble. They must especially be reminded that God is not to be found in every man. That we are not all brothers, the children of one Father. That there are not really many ways to find God. That not all spiritual experiences come from God. Again, if they understand that the opinions they hear in meetings are the untrained assessments of people trying to stay sober, not the teachings of scripture, they can maintain a realistic expectation.

These things are too difficult for some new Christians to deal with. They get upset with what they deem to be heresy. They find themselves distressed with the eternal condition of their peers in A.A. They are repeatedly involved in arguments over spiritual matters. If you have a person in this condition, it may be necessary to advise him to back off from A.A. If you do this, you must provide him with daily contact and conversation concerning God, sobriety, and emotional stability. The new person needs this accountability and opportunity for relationship. His thinking is in a state of fearful flux. He needs validation of his thoughts and feelings. Don't take away his support system without helping him find another.

DO YOU STILL GO TO THOSE MEETINGS?

One of the pitfalls of recovery through Alcoholics Anonymous is addiction to treatment. Anyone who is recovering from an obsessive behavior faces the danger of substituting a new addiction. Many is the addict who has "recovered" by pouring himself into work, religion, or golf. While these pursuits are certainly more constructive than chemical use, they still prevent the development of healthy human relationships and often interfere with proper attention to family and friends.

Most addicts come to their first meeting asking, "How long do I have to go to these meetings?" The usual response is something like, "The rest of your life." If recovery is an actual priority, the person quickly becomes immersed in the A.A. environment. In most metropolitan areas there are hundreds of meetings every week. In these meetings

> *One of the pitfalls of recovery: Addiction to treatment.*

the addict finds new friends with whom he shares much common experience. There is development of personal closeness and openness. The meeting room becomes an oasis, an escape from the stress of daily living.

In the beginning this involvement is necessary to sobriety. The new person needs a safe place to hide. As his length of sobriety increases, however, there should be a return to some semblance of normal living. Relationships outside A.A. should begin to be healed and renewed. The family will need some attention. The workplace should provide some human contact. If after a year or two the addict is still attending two meetings a day and has no outside contacts, something is wrong.

The family may still see this as a better alternative than visits to the jail and late nights of fretting and fighting. While it is admittedly better than intoxication, it is not maturity. The meeting room and the society of A.A. has become a drug. Rather than learning to deal with the difficulties inherent in daily life by experiencing them, dealing with them using the principles of the program, then seeking support and validation in meetings, the addict is running to a safe place and hiding there. If you are a spiritual helper to this person you will need to point this out and assist in a transition to real life. A few invitations to church and outside social events may be a place to start.

"I CAN'T CONFESS THAT!"

Since the 1970's the church has been gloriously reminded of the power of spoken words. The words of Jesus in **MARK 11:23** have come alive to millions.

> *and nothing will be too much for you. This mountain, for instance: Just say, 'Go jump in the lake'—no shuffling or shilly-shallying—and it's as good as done.*

(Message Bible)

> *I can guarantee this truth: This is what will be done for someone who doesn't doubt but believes what he says will happen: He can say to this mountain, 'Be uprooted and thrown into the sea,' and it will be done for him.*

(God's Word)

We have become very conscious of the words we speak. In some circles it is tantamount to heresy to "confess" that we are sick or broke or anything other than totally blessed. People in churches where this is taught have a particular problem with A.A. meetings.

In almost every meeting of Alcoholics Anonymous, participants are expected to introduce themselves with their name followed by the phrase, "I'm an alcoholic." This practice is so

> **My name is Judy and I'm an alcoholic.**

widespread as to be associated with support groups even in the media and movies. Everybody knows about it. The confession-conscious Christian, having just heard their first sermon on "The Power of the Tongue" or "You Can Have What You Say," will undoubtedly recoil at this tradition. This is indeed a problem if the individual really needs the support of an A.A. group in order to maintain sobriety.

This practice, while universal in Alcoholics Anonymous, is actually only a tradition, not a requirement. It began as an attempt to provide a place of identification for the newcomer and a place of reminder for the old-timer. New people in A.A. meetings often let down their defenses and listen when they see they are in the midst of a group of people like themselves. There is a sort of instant camaraderie. In addition, those who have been members for a while are thought to benefit by being reminded of their problem lest they forget and drink again. Remember that denial of their condition is one of the primary characteristics of most addicts. It is important for them to admit their condition and own the responsibility for their recovery. These are valid concerns for people in A.A. and deserve serious consideration.

The newcomer who is uncomfortable with confessing he is an alcoholic or an addict can rest assured that he does not have to do this in order to be a member of the group. The preamble which is read at the beginning of nearly every meeting says clearly, "The only requirement for membership is a desire to stop drinking." If you are counseling a person who needs to be in meetings but won't "confess" he is an alcoholic, then give him permission to introduce himself with his name and the phrase, "I have a desire to stop drinking." That is the only requirement.

When you dispense this information, be sure that your client's objections are genuinely spiritual and not simply an attempt to continue in his denial of his condition. If he is, in fact, an alcoholic, the condition will not be cured by his refusal to say it. **ROMANS 4:17** tells us that Abraham "...*calleth* *those things which be not as though they were."* Unfortunately, we often twist this to say *"...calleth those things that are as though they are not."* This is not biblical. It is denial. It is deadly.

My personal practice when attending meetings today, after many years of sobriety and a thorough immersion in the Charismatic Word of Faith teaching, is to tell them, "My name is Virgil and I am an alcoholic." I am able to do this very easily without fear that my confession will somehow drive me to drink or keep me bound by alcoholism. While drunkenness is one of the symptoms of the disease of alcoholism, there are many others. I no longer drink, but I am still under construction in many other areas in my thinking and emotions. In addition, the bodily predisposition to addiction is still in me. If I were to drink today I would still be alcoholic. The biggest difference between my last day of drinking and today is that today I have a choice. I am still alcoholic, but I choose not to drink.

Some folks have a problem with that, and that is their prerogative. The important thing is to be well-acquainted with the reasons for the practice and the ways to help a new Christian understand it and deal with it. It should not be allowed to become a major issue for him. The question is, "Does he need the support of the group to stay sober?" If the answer is "yes," I must try to help him navigate through the land mines of A.A. life while growing in his Christian walk.

> *The biggest difference between my last day of drinking and today is that I have a CHOICE.*

IF I'M HEALED, I WANT A DRINK!

The Christians of my most intimate acquaintance are quite avid in their proclamation that God is a Healer. We believe very adamantly that He wants to heal every sickness. Given this viewpoint it is natural for us to believe He can and will heal the alcoholic. From my own personal testimony I know this to be true. I also know that the alcoholic mind is a devious thing. It wants to believe above all else that "social" drinking will one day be an option. I know that sounds absolutely insane to those of you who are not addicts, but I assure you it is the truth. If the addict thought sanely about his chemical use he would not be an addict!

I do not believe that God delivered me and healed me in order that I might more comfortably enjoy a glass of wine. He wants me abstinent. For me to intentionally put alcohol or other sedatives in my body is to tempt the grace of God. I go so far as to avoid foods cooked with alcohol lest the molecules trigger a response in my body. Why be foolish? I occasionally eat in places where I don't know what is in the food. If I inadvertently ingest alcohol, I can usually detect it immediately by my body's reaction. My chest gets tight. I get a headache. I am sometimes short of breath and very anxious. I am happy to report that when this happens the Name of Jesus is more than sufficient to rebuke the symptoms. The new Christian and neophyte in recovery may not be so well-equipped. He may choose to drink or use drugs to make himself comfortable again.

From the spiritual standpoint, we know that addiction can be associated with demonic influence. I believe most addicts are demon-driven. When God intervenes to deliver a person from a demon, He wants that person to remain free. Jesus gave us a clear promise concerning the behavior of demons. If they leave, they will surely return:

I don't believe that God healed and delivered me so that I might enjoy a glass of wine.

MATTHEW 12:43-45

"When an evil spirit comes out of a man, it goes through arid places seeking rest and does not find it. Then it says, 'I will return to the house I left.' When it arrives, it finds the house unoccupied, swept clean and put in order. Then it goes and takes with it seven other spirits more wicked than itself, and they go in and live there. And the final condition of that man is worse than the first. That is how it will be with this wicked generation."

(New International Version)

"When a defiling evil spirit is expelled from someone, it drifts along through the desert looking for an oasis, some unsuspecting soul it can bedevil. When it doesn't find anyone, it says, 'I'll go back to my old haunt.' On return it finds the person spotlessly clean, but vacant. It then runs out and rounds up seven other spirits more evil than itself and they all move in, whooping it up. That person ends up far worse off than if he'd never gotten cleaned up in the first place. That's what this generation is like: You may think you have cleaned out the junk from your lives and gotten

ready for God, but you weren't hospitable to my kingdom message, and now all the devils are moving back in."

(Message Bible)

When a demon is cast out of a human being, it will always come back in an attempt to reoccupy its former home. When it returns, it must find out what is now occupying the old house, or body. In the case of addiction, it will attempt to determine if obsession with the drug has been replaced by something else. If you are a Christian, neither Satan nor his demons can look into your innermost being. It is off limits to them. They can, however, place thoughts in your mind to determine how you will react. They know that *"out of the abundance of the heart the mouth speaketh."* (MATTHEW 12:34)

A person who has been delivered of a demon of alcoholism can rest assured that a test is coming. Probably more than one. The demon will plant thoughts in the mind in an attempt to see what is in the heart. Whether the thoughts come as a response to a beer ad on TV or a passing thought on a hot day, the new person needs to know how to resist. He must be filled with the Word of God in order to respond in a way that discourages the demon from his mission. The responses to thoughts of temptation reveal the content of the heart and let the demonic tempters know if they have a chance to reclaim their victim. If the response includes picking up a drink, even if it is intended to be "just one," the evicted spirit returns with a crowd of his rowdy friends. To drink after being delivered is to give place to the devil in a most destructive way.

> **To drink after being delivered is to give place to the devil in a most destructive way.**

I am absolutely convinced that the Lord delivers and heals the alcoholic and the addict. The Name of Jesus is greater than any demonic force, and the stripes of Jesus are sufficient to heal any physical malady. In the case of the addict this is absolutely necessary. I am also firmly convinced that intentionally taking drugs or alcohol into the body after being delivered is to tempt the Lord. There is no need for it. It only gives place to the devil. It stirs up the physical phenomenon of craving. It all too often rekindles thoughts and desires which eventually overwhelm the addict and drive him to another bout with his addiction, a journey that is not always a round trip. Total abstinence is the only sane goal.

WHERE IS THE CHURCH?

The numbers of people impacted by addiction provide a challenge and an opportunity for the church. We surely have the responsibility to help those who are in trouble. We are Christians. In addition, we could benefit from the ignorance of the psychological and governmental agencies that are trying to respond to this epidemic in our culture. They are insisting that addicts and their families find some kind of spiritual life. Through the twelve step phenomenon people are being encouraged to reach out to some kind of "god." They are creating a great demand for some sort of spiritual reality which speaks to the need of the addict. We are in the enviable position of being the oldest and largest retailer of the product they are seeking.

Many churches have implemented wonderful programs to address this issue. To make a blanket statement concerning "the church" is to oversimplify grossly. First, there are many different branches of "the church." In addition, the response of each congregation is determined to a large extent by their background, both sociologically and doctrinally. But before we look at possibilities for positive action, we want to enumerate some common hindrances which block churches from moving effectively to meet this need.

IGNORING THE PROBLEM

The most common response of the church is no response at all. Not that most pastors don't realize there is a societal problem, they simply don't see it as a problem in their congregation. This is especially true in suburban areas where everybody looks to be doing well, at least on Sunday morning. Many of the problems generated by drug and alcohol abuse are categorized in other ways: a lack of responsibility, poor discipline of children, a need for better communication in marriages, etc. These are so much easier to believe in such a nice group of people.

Several years ago I heard a counselor make this statement: "Any household which consistently lives below their predicted economic level probably has an addiction problem somewhere." I thought this a bit simplistic at the time, but experience has caused me to broaden the search. Any home which has ongoing chaos in its finances, its relationships, and sometimes even its physical health is likely to have some obsessive behavior hidden somewhere. Be a little curious in looking at those households which seem in continual chaos. You might be surprised at the truth.

> *Any household which consistently lives below their predicted economic level probably has an addiction problem somewhere.*

Perhaps a more common form of denial is the "we teach them the Word, and that's enough" school of thought. In the Charismatic world we pride ourselves on the quality of our teaching. Many of us also like to brag about our healing and deliverance ministries. We even have special services dedicated to healing the sick and freeing the bound. Certainly, if an alcoholic or his family will come and receive this ministry, be grounded in the Word and effectively discipled, there is healing available. Unfortunately the nature of addiction almost precludes this.

The alcoholic is a very adaptable animal. He can easily hide himself in the church environment, especially when this only requires an occasional brief appearance lubricated with a smile and a friendly greeting. Although keeping his secret may require that he intimidate his family, he finds this to be a simple task. After all, they want to be accepted as a nice, normal family. They are ashamed, and shame motivates deception. They are very good at it. Reality is this: They are in your congregation. Accept it and make provision to deal with it.

IGNORANCE OF THE PROBLEM

There is a large segment of the church which is aware of the need to help addicts and their families. They see the destruction in the lives of people. They are good-hearted, loving people and have a great desire to be a blessing. They know that Jesus has an answer for these poor souls. They are particularly touched by the plight of the family, especially the children. They often find themselves ministering to the needs of these casualties of the addiction war.

Unfortunately, most churches, especially those in our Pentecostal or Charismatic flow, are peculiarly ignorant of the nature of the problem. We have been schooled to believe that these are people who are morally weak, or who simply don't want help. It is to this group that I am writing this book. I believe that Paul's declaration in **1 CORINTHIANS 9:22** speaks specifically to this problem.

"I am made all things to all men, that I might by all means save some,"

(King James)

I didn't take on their way of life. I kept my bearings in Christ—but I entered their world and tried to experience things from their point of view. I've become just about every sort of servant there is in my attempts to lead those I meet into a God-saved life. There is ministry power in being able to put yourself in someone else's shoes.

(Message Bible)

Identification with those to whom we minister is a basic tenet of the Gospel. Paul wrote to his beloved friends in Philippi:

PHILIPPIANS 2:5-8

Think of yourselves the way Christ Jesus thought of himself. He had equal status with God but didn't think so much of himself that he had to cling to the advantages of that status no matter what. Not at all. When the time came, he set aside the privileges of deity and took on the status of a slave, became human! Having become human, he stayed human. It was an incredibly humbling process. He didn't claim special privileges. Instead, he lived a selfless, obedient life and then died a selfless, obedient death—and the worst kind of death at that: a crucifixion.

(Message Bible)

He asked them to adopt the attitude of Christ who allowed Himself to identify with the plight of fallen men in order to obtain redemption for them. The beginning of effective ministry is humility leading to identification, a willingness to feel someone else's pain. In order to do this it is necessary to make an attempt to understand how the world looks through that person's eyes. It is not necessary to be an addict to help an addict. It is necessary to love an addict enough to understand an addict. We must try to grasp the problem.

IT'S NOT MY JOB

Another attitude which hinders effective Christian response to the problems of alcoholism and addiction is the tendency to abdicate responsibility. In our present society, the church has given much of her charge for the care of the broken in life over to other institutions. We much prefer to defer, especially to government and to "professionals." Many pastors and churches assume that the answer to these issues lies with government intervention. More money, more treatment centers, more social programs, more anything. Others have great faith in psychology and medicine, areas which used to be the sole province of the church. They are much more comfortable referring a troubled couple to a therapist than intervening themselves.

Reality is that the government is drowning in red ink. It cannot afford to do what it is doing now, much less do more. In addition, referral to professional counselors and treatment programs is a very expensive alternative. Many health insurances no longer cover such treatment. It is time for the church to recognize the problem, educate itself, and be courageous enough to do something about it. This doesn't mean that every Christian needs to be an expert on addiction, but it does mean that pastors need to be sure that someone in their congregation is being purposely prepared to minister in this area.

O.K., SO WHAT DO WE DO?

Since you have read this far I will assume you are convinced there is a problem. It could be that you are one who had the problem or one who loves an addict. Maybe you are a pastor or a concerned parishioner. The question for you has to be, "What can we do about the problem of alcoholism and addiction?" There are any number of possibilities. Many congregations have done effective and creative things. I assure

> *There are 3 general areas or types of ministry to the chemically dependent: Education, Intervention, and Support.*

you, any attempt to constructively address the issue will bring about an increase in the number of such cases in your church. God will give you opportunities to be a blessing as you determine to prepare yourself.

EDUCATE

Ignorance of any subject is a guarantee of ineffective action. The most basic and necessary way to address a problem is to become informed. In our day it is almost criminal to be ignorant in the area of drug and alcohol addiction, yet much of the church labors in the dark. There are many sources of information available with a minimum of effort and expense. Sometimes it seems the church finds it easier to deplore the problem than to address it. The fact you are reading this book is a positive testimony to your motivation to acquire accurate knowledge. The first thing you can do to fight the plague of addiction is to educate yourself. If you are a minister or a concerned parishioner, the place to start is with you. There are any number of good books on the subject of alcoholism. Some are listed in the bibliography. I believe the best place to start is with the Big Book called, *"Alcoholics Anonymous."* Most libraries have a copy, or you can purchase one easily through your local A.A. fellowship. You will normally find a phone number in the Yellow Pages under Alcoholism. The book reflects the nature of the thinking of an addicted person. Some of the stories in the back of the book give helpful glimpses into the warped mind-set of the drunk. The text of the book addresses many of the problems of the alcoholic and his family in an understandable way.

Allow me to address one common "Christian" fallacy. Because you have the Holy Spirit and are a good student of the Word does not necessarily equip you to deal with addicts. I'm sure you are a lovely person, but without some specific preparation you will be of little aid. If you are good-hearted and determined, you will eventually learn through experience. Unfortunately, the human cost of such experience is high. I beseech you to take the trouble to learn from those who have been in the battle before you.

> *By talking about the subject and inviting people to learn the realities of recovery, we create an atmosphere for healing.*

In my years as a pastor I have encountered many people who felt the Lord was calling them to start some kind of ministry to the addict and alcoholic. I remember one dear lady who claimed to have had a visitation from the Lord. He wanted her to open a home for young people troubled by drugs. She had no experience, no knowledge, and no resources. I encouraged her to take steps to prepare herself for this ministry and believe God that her faithfulness over small things would be rewarded by promotion in due time. I never heard any more about it. This is fairly typical. There is much to be done, but good intentions and godly desires must be transformed into effective actions. The first step is always preparation.

Another good place to learn is in an actual meeting of Alcoholics Anonymous. There are many meetings which are open to the public. You can call the local office and ask for the time and place of what is known as an "open" meeting. You will be welcome in this setting to observe and learn. In addition to A.A. meetings, most larger cities have some form of mission ministry in the inner city. They would probably love to show you around and allow you to help out in some of their services or activities. Generally speaking, people who have quietly given their lives to helping addicts will be a great source of information about the daily realities of this ministry.

Nearly every community now has some organization dedicated to educating the public about alcoholism and/or drug addiction. These folks can usually be located in the Yellow Pages and will often provide a pile of free literature. If they don't exist in your town, try dialing "information" in the state capital. They are out there and waiting to hear from you. Many have regular newsletters which will advertise educational seminars throughout the year. The resources are immense for those who want to learn.

In addition to educating yourself, you can help to educate your church. If you have a book store, make material available for purchase. Check the bibliography for ideas. Bring in speakers. If you can't bring yourself to do it on Sunday morning, sponsor a workshop or special seminar on the subject. You will be shocked at the turnout. There are many resources available. I have invited counselors from local treatment centers with excellent results. One of my church members was an alcohol counselor. His teaching on the basics of alcoholism became a very popular tape series.

When inviting speakers to help addicts and their families, avoid the temptation to bring in someone who leans heavily on a great testimony of deliverance. While this may be encouraging and exciting, without some substance in the principles of healing and deliverance there will be little long-term benefit. Look for speakers with experience in treating addictions as well as in living them.

By talking about the subject and inviting people to learn the realities of recovery, we create an atmosphere for healing. Although we are saved by grace and can stand only because of the blood of Jesus, the church is often the most shame-filled place in town. We must break through the mentality which says, "No one at the church must know," and replace it with, "If I can only get to church I can share my burden with my family." As we make a conscious effort to acknowledge the problem and take positive steps to minister to those affected, we open the arms of Jesus to those who are bound. We offer them the freedom to reach out for help without fear of being castigated and shunned.

Probably the most important area of education is in the children's

> *Education in the children's department is important. This is the place where we can actually do something to prevent the disaster rather than clean up after it.*

department. This is the place where we can actually do something to prevent the disaster rather than clean up after it. It is important to address the issue with youth, but that comes a little too late in our current social milieu. By the time most kids get to the youth group they have already been faced with a decision about drugs and alcohol. Children are exposed to chemical use at a disturbingly early age. They need to have accurate facts rather than parental fears on which to base their choices. Unlike the public schools, we are not constrained to present the subject without interjecting values. We have the privilege of instructing the kids about God's opinion. What better place to learn?

Some parents will be disturbed at the idea of "exposing" little Petunia to such things. Keep an eye on these parents. They are headed for trouble. You must, however, lovingly give them the option to hold their kids out of these sessions. Other parents will be distraught because they feel threatened. If Billy Boy knows the truth about drinking and smoking, he will recognize the hypocrisy in his parents when they drag him to church, then go home and hit the liquor cabinet. If we find situations like this among our so-called "Christian" families, we are constrained to do something to intervene. The best way I know to raise a rebellious child who despises God and the church is to espouse one thing and live another.

One real advantage to instructing children about alcohol and drugs is the opportunity to uncover hidden addiction problems. Several years ago I had the privilege of representing a treatment facility in its public relations program. I went to local schools and spoke to classes. Even though the kids were as young as 9, they were quite capable of understanding the problem. In every class there were some children who reacted to the content by putting their heads down on their desks or covering their ears. When I inquired with the teachers I found in every case that there was a problem in the home. Shouldn't the church be interested in this kind of information? God help us if we're not.

INTERVENE

One question frequently asked by concerned relatives, friends, and ministers is, "What can we do to make him (her) stop drinking?" For the church that wants to go beyond the simple dispersion of information there is another level of involvement: intervention. This means some form of active effort to confront the behavior of the alcoholic and force him to positive action. This is a bit daring for most churches. Most of us prefer the passive presentation of theory. It's much less messy.

One of the most common places where active addicts come in contact with the church is in the distress of a relative, often a wife. The scene is familiar to all pastors. A woman comes in to the office with any one of a number of complaints. She may simply be concerned about wayward children. She may complain of her husband's lack of spiritual leadership. She may even relate a history of physical

> *Intervention: some form of active effort to confront the behavior of the alcoholic and force him to positive action.*

abuse. After a little questioning the pastor discovers a pattern of alcohol or drug abuse. Now what?

I came to the conclusion a few years ago that I had a responsibility to my flock to deal with people who profess to be part of the congregation and are living in ways which are overtly destructive to the church or to their family. In the case of alcoholism and addiction this means confronting the issue. If the abuser doesn't claim to be a Christian then I must try to help my parishioner get in touch with someone who can guide him in the process of dealing with an addict in the home. In either case, something must be done to help both the family and the addict.

There is an old adage that a drunk has to "reach bottom" before he can get help. The idea is that no one will do the things necessary for sobriety until they are motivated by the enormity of their own misery or necessity. This is true. Unfortunately, many die or cause immense destruction before they reach a bottom on their own. We have an obligation to bring the bottom up to meet them. I mean it is our responsibility to make some effort to increase the discomfort the addict is experiencing.

> *"Bottom-raising" can be a difficult task.*

Bottom-raising can be a difficult task, but there are resources available. Some years ago we had the opportunity to help in what the treatment community refers to as an "intervention." This basically means getting a number of significant people to simultaneously confront the addict and insist that he get help. In our case, the man was a member of our church. His wife reported numerous instances of drunk driving and other frightening behaviors. We knew there was a problem because we had smelled alcohol on his breath at church functions. We enlisted the help of treatment professionals and embarked on a new adventure.

The first step was recruiting allies. This meant talking to people who were close to our subject. We'll call him Tip. Anyone who was dear to Tip was fair game. We needed people who had first-hand experience of the effects of his drinking: friends, co-workers, relatives. Many had anecdotes to relate, but few were willing to participate. They didn't want to call good old Tip an alcoholic. Some had to be informed about the nature of alcoholism and the purpose of treatment. Finally we had a group of five. Now we had to get organized.

With the help of a professional counselor, we each compiled a list of specific instances when Tip's drinking had caused us grief. A child's fear at daddy being passed out. A wife's chagrin at forgotten appointments. A sister's panic in a drunken car ride. Each one listed as many specific incidents as they could remember. Then each incident was rewritten to be as non-accusatory and matter-of-fact as possible. "Dad, I was really scared and cold when you got drunk and forgot to pick me up from school. One day I stood in the snow until dark and you never came. I cried until a stranger called mom at work." "Tip, I was really hurt and embarrassed when you came to the family reunion drunk. You called me names then passed out on the dinner table. We were all too embarrassed to wake you up."

We went through every incident with the counselor. She helped us decide which ones to use and which ones to leave out. She coached us on language to emphasize the pain caused by the behavior and the connection to drinking. It was a difficult process. Then we started the hard part.

Our counselor now took us through a practice intervention. One person pretended to be Tip while the others took turns speaking to him. The premise of the upcoming meeting was this: Tip would be brought into the room under false pretenses. He would be shocked to see us. We would have a seat reserved for him, preferably not near the door. After he was seated we would each tell him how much we loved him and that we were there because of our concern for him. The counselor would tell him what was going to happen: "Each of these people who care for you have some things they want to say. We would like for you to listen before you respond. You may get angry. That is OK. Just try to hear what is being said."

The introductions made, the process begins. Each person in turn reads his statements. In the practice session, the mock-Tip tries to attack— calling names, yelling, crying. The goal is to prepare the participants to remain calm in the face of Tip's anger and defensiveness. This practice time is very important. We want to have a confrontation, not an explosion. It is vital to prepare a calm, loving atmosphere. The content is threatening enough without attitudes to match. Bitterness and pain must be identified and talked about now, before the real drama begins.

After practicing the content, we practiced the conclusion. The goal of the intervention is to get Tip into treatment for his addiction. The counselor has already made arrangements for him to be admitted to a treatment center the very day of the meeting. His wife will have his bag packed and in the car. A plane ticket is purchased in his name. His job is ready to cooperate. The moment Tip sees that his drinking is causing trouble we can press him to do something immediately.

Each person must now be ready to be in agreement on the bottom line. What are we asking him to do? What will be the consequences for Tip if he ignores our concerns? Will his wife leave him? Will his nieces no longer come to visit? Will his job take him back? In this case we determined to establish a "fall-back" position. If Tip

> *The goal of intervention: To get the alcoholic/addict into treatment for his addiction.*

insists he can quit on his own we will give him that opportunity, but he must agree that any alcohol intake within the next year will mean he goes to treatment immediately. We were ready.

Tip came in the company of his sister. He was shocked to see the room full of people. He was moderately defensive and got angry a few times. He cried and denied, but finally agreed to plan B. He went to treatment after another drinking bout. My thought at the time was, "Wouldn't it be nice if the church could love people enough to go through this kind of discomfort to try and save them." I believe the church can do this. It is painful and uncomfortable, but it is life-saving.

The principles involved in this process are applicable in the church.

Jesus told us in **MATTHEW 18:15-17**:

> *"If a believer does something wrong, go, confront him when*
> *the two of you are alone. If he listens to you, you have won*
> *back that believer. But if he does not listen, take one or two*
> *others with you so that every accusation may be verified*
> *by two or three witnesses. If he ignores these witnesses,*
> *tell it to the community of believers. If he also ignores the*
> *community, deal with him as you would a heathen or a tax*
> *collector.*

(God's Word)

The principle of dealing with a sinning brother is very clear. The requirements are that he be confronted individually first, then with a witness. The final step is to bring him into confrontation with the "church." My belief is that we can apply this principle to anyone who claims to be a Christian. If you love an alcoholic, you can begin the process by asking him to stop drinking. If he refuses, go to your pastor for further instruction.

The key principles in the process are simple: recognize, recruit, organize, confront, and follow through. We first assure ourselves we are dealing with a chemical problem. We then recruit as many significant people as we can locate. Especially important are people in positions of authority or who hold particular esteem in the eyes of the subject. Parents, teachers, employers, or supervisors–anyone who has leverage. After recruitment comes the crucial phase of preparation. This is key to success. Finally comes the moment of truth: confrontation in an attitude of love.

> **Key principles**
> **in the process:**
> **Recognize**
> **Recruit**
> **Organize**
> **Confront**
> **Follow-through**

There is one hidden principle here. You need an outside guide who is not emotionally involved. Let me make this clear: don't try this on your own. If you are a relative of an addict, talk to your pastor. If he doesn't know what you are talking about call the local alcoholism council. If all else fails, write us and we will find you a good referral. You need someone to guide you through the process. If you are a pastor, call your local alcoholism council. Simply tell them you want to know more about intervention. You need to know how to do this.

SUPPORT

I thank God for every church which is educating its people on the subject of addiction. I am grateful for every pastor who is trying to equip himself to help the alcoholic. It is music to my ears to hear that some brave pastor has helped organize an intervention. We take seminars on the subject to churches and are thrilled when people come to be informed. What blesses even more, however, is when a church takes the information and begins to formulate ongoing programs of support for the addict and his family.

By educating we make it possible for people to identify potential problems in themselves and others. In intervention we attempt to propel an individual abuser into a treatment setting. At this level we are still expecting the addict to receive support and ongoing care in the world's mechanisms. We are sort of "sending him out" like we would dry clean a suit. The church which really wants to mobilize resources in the area of addiction can take strides to provide a network of support and healing for family and addict alike. When you think

Shouldn't the church be the most natural place to find a "support" group?

about it, isn't the church the most natural place to find a "support" group?

If the pastor feels he cannot devote his own time to specializing in the support of addicts and their families, he can appoint someone from the congregation to oversee the ministry. Send him to seminars and provide him with educational materials. Someone needs to be competent in the field and identified as the one who operates in that ministry. This makes it safe for families to begin to shed their masks. An atmosphere of acceptance is essential for healing to take place. For the person who is just getting out of treatment, a church with some idea of the nature of his problem can be a welcome haven. He needs a place which has someone to help him deal with the problems of being a Christian in recovery, someone familiar with addiction, treatment, and A.A., in addition to being a strong Bible student.

Going further with the idea of providing support, the church can open its facilities to support groups. There are often A.A. groups in need of a place to meet. Churches are a favorite setting. This is one method of getting recovering addicts inside the church building. The two most obvious groups are Alcoholics Anonymous and its sister organization for family members, Alanon. While neither of these groups is expressly Christian, the simple fact of meeting in a church has a sanctifying effect on the participants. It also provides a familiar place for church members to come for their necessary meetings.

Another option for support is the founding of overtly Christian support groups. There are several nationwide. You will find a listing in the Appendix. All of these groups are full of wonderful, dedicated, Christian people. They can provide you with literature and ideas for establishing a group.

While I strongly advocate using the resources already available, there are other options. You can start your own in-house program of support for addicts and/or their families. This can be a daunting project if you have no experience or guidance, but it need not be a catastrophe. The first step is to determine interest. Need is not a problem, but many who need it won't come until the program has become established. You must locate the willing few.

The best way to locate the willing is to sponsor a seminar on the subject. Bring in an outside speaker who will present the principles of recovery as outlined in this book, or use a staff member who is trained and familiar with the topic. Advertise well in advance and put the meeting on a Saturday or an evening when there is no regular service. This allows for a crowd specifically interested in the topic. At the conclusion of the seminar, distribute an anonymous questionnaire to evaluate the material. Include in the questionnaire a place to indicate interest in two support groups, one for addicts and one for their families.

To actually begin the group, start with a well-trained leader. Select someone with a firm Christian foundation and a compassion for people. He should be familiar with the material in this book, and he should certainly attend a few A.A. and Alanon meetings to get a feel for the clientele. Schedule the meetings on an off night for the church to avoid the potential embarrassment of being seen by other Christians. Set a predetermined number of meetings for the group, usually twelve weeks. This gives a sense of finitude to the activity and gives people hope. At the last meeting a schedule may be set for another cycle or for other groups which may spring up out of the first.

The first meeting should have an informational tone along with some "get acquainted" activities. Review the plan for the remainder of the meetings and let the leader share his or her testimony. Set ground rules for the group. All meetings should keep to ninety minutes or less and be opened and closed with prayer. Discussions will be moderated by the leader as the designee of the Pastor. Determine what language will be allowed. Emphasize the confidentiality of the group. This is an absolute essential. Other meetings should follow some discussion guide which allows for reading, prayer and preparation at home.

A review of the many different programs of recovery available today has led me to a list of general principles which are essential for a solid sobriety. These "Seven Principles of Recovery" make a good outline for discussion in meetings. Briefly stated, the principles are:

1. *Absolute deflation.*

> An admission of defeat and a cry for help, recognizing the nature of addiction and becoming willing to do whatever is necessary to recover.

2. *Faith in God.*

> A beginning of willingness to acknowledge a divine being and taking steps to know Him.

3. *Accountability.*

> Establishing accountable relationships with personal mentors, group support, and church involvement.

4. *Self-examination.*

> Developing a rigorous, structured, honest method of reflecting one's behavior and motives. Change is the opposite of death.

5. *Restitution and restoration.*

> God has forgotten our sins, but human relations must be repaired.

6. *Commitment to ongoing spiritual growth.*

> Establishing the spiritual life as a lifestyle through church involvement, prayer, and Bible study.

7. *Service to others.*

You can't keep what you don't give away.

A TWELVE WEEK GROUP MIGHT GO LIKE THIS:

Week 1:	*Introduction and get acquainted time*
Week 2:	*Principle 1*
Week 3:	*Principle 1*
Week 4:	*Principle 2*
Week 5:	*Principle 3*
Week 6:	*Principle 3*
Week 7:	*Principle 4*
Week 8:	*Principle 4*
Week 9:	*Principle 5*
Week 10:	*Principle 6*
Week 11:	*Principle 7*
Week 12:	*Wrap-up and evaluation*

The companion workbook, *"Seven Principles of Recovery,"* which is dedicated to these seven principles can be used by an individual in recovery, by a counselor, or as a group discussion guide. If you are leading a group, give the workbook to the group members at the first meeting. Have them prepare ahead of time. Then, in discussion, ask for questions or areas of difficulty. Hone in on principles and problems. You will have more than enough to talk about.

If you are a pastor with a parishioner in trouble, you can use the workbook as a tool in counseling. Work through each segment with him. Be tough and exacting. He can become a valued member of your church and he can teach you much in the process. If you are in need of recovery, be diligent in the doing of the work in the workbook. Don't drink, don't use, and ask God for help. You are in for an adventure.

We have also found that the principles outlined above and the questions in the workbook are very helpful to family members. Don't hesitate to use the material on any compulsive behavior, even compulsive involvement in abusive relationships. God's Word works on everybody if they are willing to be honest.

There is much more that could be said. Science is finding new information daily. Psychology is formulating new patterns for treatment. In the meantime, however, our communities are full of suffering people. God has provided us with answers and opportunities. I hope this little book is of use to you as you seek to find freedom or to help those who are bound. I will close this section with the scripture which God used to encourage me when I was just beginning my journey:

PSALM 116:3-9

The sorrows of death compassed me, and the pains of hell gat hold upon me: I found trouble and sorrow. Then called I upon the name of the LORD; O LORD, I beseech thee, deliver my soul. Gracious is the LORD, and righteous; yea, our God is merciful. The LORD preserveth the simple: I was brought low, and he helped me. Return unto thy rest, O my soul; for the LORD hath dealt bountifully with thee. For thou hast delivered my soul from death, mine eyes from tears, and my feet from falling. I will walk before the LORD in the land of the living.

(King James Version)

APPENDIX

SUGGESTED READING

1. *Alcoholics Anonymous* (The Big Book) Third Edition Alcoholics Anonymous World Services, Inc, New York, 1976.

2. *Serenity, A Companion for 12 Step Recovery,* Thomas Nelson Publishers.

3. *The Basic Text,* Narcotics Anonymous.

4. *Gamblers Anonymous - Sharing Recovery Through Gamblers Anonymous* (ISBN 0-917839-00-5).

5. *Gamblers Anonymous - A New Beginning.*

6. Joe McQueen, *The Steps We Took.*

7. Melodie Beattie, *Codependent No More: How to Stop Controlling Others and Start Caring for Yourself.*

8. *The 12 Steps-A Spiritual Journey (a working guide to healing damaged emotions)* [ISBN 0-941405-44-3].

9. *The 12 Steps for Christians* [ISBN 0-941405-57-5].

10. *Prayers for the 12 Steps-A Spiritual Journey* [ISBN 0-941405-28-1].

11. *The Life Recovery Bible,* [ISBN 0-8423-2809-2] (excellent for anyone in recovery).

12. *Living Free* (a guide to forming recovery ministries, written for pastors and church leaders) [ISBN 0-941405-16-8].

13. *The 12 Steps--A Way Out* (Focuses on issues common to people raised in troubled homes) [ISBN 0-941405-11-7].

14. *The 12 Steps for Adult Children* [ISBN 0-941405-08-7].

15. *Overeaters Anonymous – OA.*

16. William Backus & Marie Chapian, *Telling Yourself the Truth.*

17. Paul Meier, M.D., *Don't Let Jerks Get the Best of You* (Thomas Nelson Publishers, Nashville).

18. Frank Minirth & Paul Meier, *Happiness is a Choice*.

19. Frank Minirth, et.al., *Love Hunger*.

20. Vernon E. Johnson, *I'll Quit Tomorrow* [ISBN 0-06-250430-4].

21. Anderson Spickard, M.D. & Barbara R. Thompson, *Dying for a Drink*.

22. Robert S. McGee, *The Search for Significance* (Rapha Publishing, Houston) [ISBN 0- 945276-07-9].

23. Pat Springle, *Codependency*.

24. McGee, Springle, & Joiner, *Rapha's 12-Step Program for Overcoming Chemical Dependency*.

THE TWELVE STEPS OF ALCOHOLICS ANONYMOUS

1. *We admitted that we were powerless over alcohol - that our lives had become unmanageable.*

2. *Came to believe that a Power greater than ourselves could restore us to sanity.*

3. *Made a decision to turn our will and our lives over to the care of God as we understood Him.*

4. *Made a searching and fearless moral inventory of ourselves.*

5. *Admitted to God, to ourselves, and to another human being the exact nature of our wrongs.*

6. *Became entirely ready to have God remove all these defects of character.*

7. *Humbly asked Him to remove our shortcomings.*

8. *Made a list of all persons we had harmed and became willing to make amends to them all.*

9. *Made direct amends to such people whenever possible, except when to do so would injure them or others.*

10. *Continued to take personal inventory and when we were wrong promptly admitted it.*

11. *Sought through prayer and meditation to improve our conscious contact with God as we understood Him, praying only for the knowledge of His will for us and the power to carry that out.*

12. *Having had a spiritual awakening as the result of these steps, we tried to carry this message to alcoholics, and to practice these principles in all our affairs.*

SEVEN PRINCIPLES OF RECOVERY

The following are principles necessary to the recovery of any addict:

1. **Deflation:**   Admission - Desperation - Willingness

   Admission: This is the destruction of the alibi system, a break down of denial.

   Desperation: This is the end of hope in self-effort and ability.

   Willingness: The motivation to take difficult action which comes from the awareness that there are no alternatives or compromises.

2. **Faith in God:**   Dependence on God, not self. Prayer and Bible study.

3. **Accountability:** Development of internal controls.

4. **Self-examination**

5. **Restitution and restoration:** Without these steps repentance is a mental exercise, not a spiritual reality.

6. **Committed to ongoing spiritual growth:** Church!

7. **Service to others**

ABOUT THE AUTHOR
VIRGIL L. STOKES

Rev. Virgil L. Stokes is a graduate of the University of Oklahoma and worked for several years as a Registered Nurse in the mental health field. He is experienced in working with troubled adolescents, the mentally ill, and the chemically dependent. Having personally experienced the ravages of alcoholism, as a recovered alcoholic/addict, and the power of God to deliver, he brings special insight and revelation to this much-debated issue.

Virgil, and his wife Judy, have been in ministry since 1980. They have served four churches as pastors. They are both graduates of Rhema Bible Training Center and are ordained by Faith Christian Fellowship, International, for whom they serve as field representatives. From 1985 until 1995 they served as pastors of Living Water Faith Fellowship in Oneonta, NY before moving to Arizona. They are now pastors of Faith Christian Fellowship of Tucson, Arizona.

The Stokeses are founders of Abundant Heart Ministries, a missionary/evangelistic association involved in training pastors and church leaders at home and abroad. They also founded Faith Ministry Training Institute in Tucson, Arizona. Training programs now exist in Mexico, Panama, and on Indian Reservations in the United States. Abundant Heart's schools are designed to move Christians from the pew into the Harvest. In addition, the Stokeses write and publish printed materials in English and Spanish, especially designed to help ministers become more effective.

Rev. Stokes is deeply committed to strengthening local churches. He sees the local church as the key element in God's plan for reaching the world and is committed to encouraging the church to partake of the supernatural power deposited in her through the Holy Spirit while remaining faithful to the revealed truth of God's Word.

Faith Christian Fellowship of Tucson
P.O. Box 89156 • Tucson, AZ 85752

Phone: (520) 792-3238

E-mail: virgil@fcftucson.org • **Web Site:** www.fcftucson.org

1550214R0

Printed in Great Britain by
Amazon.co.uk, Ltd.,
Marston Gate.